In the postwar years, every Tom, Dick and Harry was flying his own airplane in pursuit of life, liberty, and freedom from gravity. A hop over the High Sierras in our Cessna One Eighty. We were at 14,500 feet en route to Death Valley Airport (211 feet below sea level), Sept 5, 1967.

Revised edition April 2014

HIGH JINKS, LOW HOPS

A Memoir of Postwar Flying

ROBERT J HING

ACKNOWLEDGMENTS

Thanks to Carolyn Zimmerman and Lily Lewin for their
assistance and encouragement

DEDICATION

To Daedalus, the legendary artificer, who made a pair of wings and flew from Crete to Sicily; and to the late Bill Cahill and Earl Magnus, who built and flew homebuilt airplanes at Clow Airport, Illinois, in the early 1970s.

AUTHOR'S NOTE

It was Bluebottle (Chapter 4) who framed the essential question: How on earth or in the sky does one spend half a lifetime?

CONTENTS

LIST OF ILLUSTRATIONS AND MAPS

WHEN THE GOING WAS GOOD

Everyone was flying personal airplanes in those years, everyone who wanted to. Aeronca, Beech, Cessna, Ercoupe, Piper, Stinson, Taylorcraft, (Auster, Miles, and DeHavilland in the UK; Beaver, Fleet, and Norseman in Canada)…those were the airplanes people flew. Maybe a couple million people at one time or other in North America, half of whom actually got some sort of a pilot's license if only student status; as many or more who took a few flips in an airplane. At the peak, there were two hundred fifty thousand personal airplanes (a cumulative number) and 20,000 airfields and landing strips. A critical mass, if you like. Gasoline was cheap; airplanes were affordable, regulation was light, enthusiasm was sky-high. It was an era unlikely to be repeated.

Our common condition, that we earthlings are prisoners of gravity, was no longer tolerated as the controlling fact of human existence. Even the dullest minds acknowledged that *bird envy*, not human nakedness (as in Adam & Eve), was our deepest hang-up.

The conquest of the air took a hundred years. Thanks, Wilbur and Orville! Thanks, Bleriot, and all the other pioneers! Then came the postwar boom, 1946 to 1980 (and a bit further), and every Tom, Dick and Harry was piloting his own airplane in pursuit of life, liberty and freedom from gravity. I was one of that merry crew.

Grassroots aviation: Fly Baby N3685, Lombard Illinois, 1973. I spent 18 months building this airplane and overhauling the engine – an utterly absorbing project. Then came the exhilaration of the first flight and all too soon my return to earth, when I once again shared the perspective of a field mouse, which can't see over the tops of things. Looking on is Al Neunteufel, who lost his life in the crash of his homebuilt airplane, 1974.

1

OUTWITTING GRAVITY

No more brilliant idea has surfaced in the muddled and murky history of thought than the theory of flight; no proof so convincing as seeing an airplane fly. It's no coincidence that Edward Abbott, who railed against gravity in his 1884 satire *Flatland*, was a contemporary of Alphonse Penaud, inventor of the rubber-powered model airplane that inspired the Wright brothers. The concept was ingenious: to use the stored energy of a rubber band to power a propeller-driven flying machine. What's more, the configuration of Penaud's model airplane ("consisting of mainplanes with dihedral tips, a tailplane, a vertical rudder and a rear pusher propeller, the whole having inherent stability both lateral and longitudinal") is credited by the historian Gibbs-Smith as being "one of the chief ancestors of the modern airplane."

Model airplanes were at one time the chief interest of my brother and me. We exulted in the flight of these tiny flying machines; to watch one go out of sight was our greatest hope – something always imminent, never realized. Why then did piloted airplanes stay aloft? It had something – everything – to do with the high spirits of the pilots. (This is a hypothesis that I still nurse.) We built these models out of balsa and glue on the living room floor. Sometimes the production line was interrupted. My special pride, a flying model of the Piper Cub, I somehow left on an armchair which my sister sat on, demolishing the airplane. But we got some of them to fly, and in flying these Lilliputian airplanes we experienced the essence of flight – lift-off and sustained flight – if only for fifteen long seconds.

There was Abbott and there was Penaud – and there was Bert. Bert sold model airplane supplies at a stall adjacent to the greengrocery in the High Street. If Penaud was the fountainhead of aeronautical theory, Bert was high priest – and my brother and I, acolytes. Bert's market stall was the temple of flight, and its peculiar incense was the uneasy mix of smells of airplane dope and fresh fruit and vegetables. We were enthusiasts, my brother and I, likely to be at the temple before Bert arrived on his pedal bike. Bert – a small man in a chargehand's white coat – affected a Druidical manner towards us in indulging our schoolboy questions and meager spending budgets. But I think he relished the role of infallible dispenser of aeronautical knowledge. Then one day my brother, straying from the received wisdom of rubber band technology, asked Bert what was the rated thrust of the Jetex 50 micro rocket motor? Bert gave him an injured look that said, this is outside our syllabus. Then he formulated his reply. "Why do you want to know?"

This rebuff encouraged us to switch our allegiance (in respect to the quest for aeronautical knowledge) to the Science Museum in South Kensington, to study, as intently as first-year ornithology students, the airplanes suspended from the ceiling there.

2

TEACH YOURSELF TO FLY

In those days – the late 1940s – airplanes were still marvelous things. The drone of an approaching plane would precipitate my headlong rush outside to glimpse the low-flying machine before it disappeared behind the houses.

At age fifteen I was inducted into my school's unit of the Air Training Corps. This was a sort of feeder organization to the RAF, which in the recent war had seen its personnel balloon to 1.2 million, and whose precipitous post-war downsizing was slowed by the Berlin blockade and the Cold War. Over the three years, 1950 – 1952, I flew in half a dozen types of aircraft at various RAF aerodromes for "air experience." (Whether these flights were a provocation to the Red Hordes, I doubt.) The twin-engine Avro Anson, introduced in 1938, was one such trusty school horse; "Faithful Annie" she was called. Eleven thousand of them were built for various duties; reeking of gasoline they would trundle us around Blackpool or wherever, and then, after landing disembark us and leave the up-chuck for the ground crew to hose down. For aerobatic flight in a Tiger Moth, the long-suffering ground crew would repack any parachute that a careless cadet, such as myself, had tinkered with and pulled the ripcord by mistake – and didn't have a half crown to pay the customary fine.

But when would we get our hands on the controls? To actually fly? In 1951, the C.O. of our unit sent some of us on a gliding course to RAF Colerne, in Wiltshire. Training was on the "teach-yourself" principle; dual instruction was not available. A knockoff of a 1926 design by Alex Lippisch was employed, the "Primary Eton". For lesson one, this most basic of gliders was suspended, facing the wind, from a German-invented tripod while the trainee pilot manipulated stick and rudder, attempting to balance the glider in the airstream. Then some very low flights were made in the Eton by means of "bungee" launches (a half-dozen cadets pulling on each end of an elastic catapult). The third stage was the winch-launched, single-seat Kirby Cadet, flown through a progression of "ground slides, airborne slides, low hops and high hops." Turns, let alone circuits, were not contemplated at this stage. (Somehow the straight-away principle of the nearby Roman roads had infiltrated the air curriculum.)

Once launched into the air, each in his turn, we apprentice pilots were guided by a bat man, as on an aircraft carrier. If, after release from the winch cable, the student held the nose high, inviting a stall (at around 25 mph), the batman would frantically beat the ground with both bats, imploring the novice airman to lower the nose and build up flying speed. It didn't work. Both of our Kirby Cadets crashed. The first glider stalled and fell off sideways – I was standing by the winch, with the glider practically overhead – and struck the ground, wing tip first, which absorbed most of the shock. Though the glider was demolished, the novice pilot got away with a broken ankle. When the next student dove in from a straight-ahead stall, he was taken away in an ambulance with a broken back, and that particular course was disbanded. (An unconscious fear of stalling stayed with me for years, so that my default landing mode was an over-fast approach.)

At the end of the year the C.O. of our school cadet corps, Sqn. Ldr. "Jack" Orr, nominated me to learn to fly the 1932-era Tiger Moth.

Photo: Cliff Hilditch

Ch. 3. White Waltham, 1952. My first-solo aircraft awaiting an engine change. Note automatic anti-stall slats on leading edge of upper mainplanes, and petrol tank in center section. G-AIRK was built 1939, still active 2007. The Moth family dated from 1925 with the first reliable, affordable light airplane. Exponents of the Moth "between the wars" included Jean Batten (the "Garbo of the Skies") and Francis Chichester, both famous for their long-distance flights. Some 8,500 Moths served as trainers in WW2.

3

THE TIGER MOTH

Santos-Dumont, also known as "Little Santos," ushered in the age of personal flight long before de Havilland in England or Taylor and Piper in America. Santos, in his airship or in one of his small airplanes, would land in the garden of one or other of his Parisian friends for lunch, or cheekily circle the Eiffel tower. One of those airplanes was the Demoiselle of 1907, "the first light plane." When a replica was made for the film "Those Magnificent Men in their Flying Machines," a small pilot, as small as Little Santos, was required, and Joan Hughes was found to fill the bill. I mention this because Joan taught me to fly, and because I've come to think of Santos-Dumont as an exponent of flight for its own sake, rather than for the purposes of commerce or war, or just to flaunt an expensive gadget.

Be that as it may, Joan Hughes was Chief Flying Instructor of the West London Aero Club, which was, and is still, tucked into a corner of the large grass aerodrome at White Waltham. When I arrived there, barely seventeen years old, on 26 July 1952, I left my bicycle behind the clubhouse, which fronted on some old tarpaulin hangars and a row of Moth biplanes. Joan wasted no time in explaining the features of the de Havilland Tiger Moth, an unmistakable aeroplane with its top mainplane set high and its tail, with spade-shaped rudder, resting on the rear skid. Miss Hughes (one did not call her Joan to her face) was a well-known pilot in England; during the War, she had been a ferry pilot, with the rank of Flight Captain, checked out on every type of aircraft. She was slight in build, as I've said. She rarely or never smiled. There is an iconic photograph of her standing on the tarmac under the nose of a giant Short Stirling bomber which towers over her like a sky-scraper. No, truly. Search out this image if you haven't seen it.

With two hundred acres of grass, allowing takeoff and landing in any direction, White Waltham aerodrome was nicely suited to the Tiger Moth, which was designed for takeoff and landing directly into the wind, according to the indication of the windsock. The Tiger Moth was not fitted with flaps, so if one approached to land too high, he had to slip the airplane to lose excess height, or open the throttle to "go round again." The Moth was then brought in to a three-point landing, on main wheels and tail skid, with the control stick fully back to stall the wings.

After ten hours instruction, which included "circuits and bumps," sideslips and spins, it was time to go solo. A lineman pulled over the prop to start the engine. I pushed the goggles over my eyes, taxied out, and rammed the throttle forward. Pop. Pop. Pop. (…fuel mixture too lean.) Then the engine settled down to a loud snarl. The airplane vibrated. It bumped across the grass. The wind rushed through the wires. Momentarily, I wished Joan was in the now-empty front cockpit. Then I was in the air. The Moth skidded through the sky, the big rudder waggling in the slipstream. (Taking off in a Tiger Moth was strangely similar to galloping a horse – only then you rose into the air, like Pegasus.)

We practiced forced landings in nearby farm fields. We side-slipped and looped and spun in furtherance of Joan's obligation to demonstrate to her young charge that an airplane is not a "house with wings." Joan switched off the engine in flight, and when the propeller stopped wind-milling, dove steeply to restart the engine. As soon as I could I played hooky and flew away from the airfield boundary. I could smell the paint factory as I glided down towards my house. A burst of power brought my siblings into the garden. "What do you want for tea, Bob?" shouted my sister (so she told me later). Returning to the aerodrome, I taxied fast towards the pumps, and the plane's momentum carried her on to the tarmac apron, down the slight gradient towards the perimeter fence. The Moth had no brakes. I had to stop her. I wrenched out the harness pin, clambered out of the cockpit, and rushed round to the front of the (big) biplane to push her to a stop. Then I realized I had better switch off the engine (the switches were on the outside of the cockpit), and I clambered on to the lower port mainplane – barely missing the propeller disc – to get at those switches.

The fact is I was wary of the Tiger Moth. In my view, flying it solo was rather like riding a jittery horse which might unseat me at any moment. Yet I relished the precariousness of flying a solo cross country to my boarding school on the North Downs (I was a scholarship boy at Lord Wandsworth College), piloting the Moth over this Domesday country, where all the fields had names: Ridge Furlong, Sheephouse, Yoke-up-Hyde and the like. Cross-country flying, an important part of the course, consisted of triangular-leg flights, with each leg about twenty miles. These training flights were mainly NW or NE from White Waltham, toward Oxford or Cambridge, but never east toward London, or, for some reason, to the South. There were only so many grass aerodromes in this flight area that could accommodate the Tiger Moth, which had to land on grass, and directly into the wind. Luton, Thame, Woodley/Reading, and Cambridge fit these specifications.

We used quarter-million scale charts, which had to be kept tightly folded or they would blow out of the cockpit. The magnetic compass was a large RAF "P" type, the size of a fish bowl. The longest cross-country I made was from White Waltham to Cambridge with an intermediate landing at Luton. The three legs totaled 135 miles, and I logged 1 hr 45 mins. flight time. (But this time must have been incorrectly recorded because the Moth cruised at barely 80 mph, and could not have gone the distance and made three take-offs and three landings in the time noted.) This was, of course, helmet and goggles flying, and, I recall, we wore sheepskin jackets – even in "summer." And concerning Cambridge, author David Garnett wrote an account of learning to fly there, at this same "Marshall's Aerodrome" in the early 1930s. The middle-aged literatus surprised himself. He wrote, "I was drunk with air. I was wild, and driving home sang and shouted."

At that time, in the early 1950s, one needed to keep a sharp lookout entering the flight pattern at White Waltham, as the airfield was shared with the RAF and Fairey Aviation, who built planes for the Fleet Air Arm. There was always activity: our Club planes, Navy planes, a Spitfire, or a Mosquito in the circuit, and a foreign chap who flick-rolled a Bucker biplane at a height of about fifty feet – or less? His plane had three airspeed indicators, and his name was Count Cantacuzene, said to be descended from the last of the Byzantine emperors. Actually, he was a Rumanian air ace who had downed Russian, German, and USAAF aircraft. (Oil-rich Rumania had a changing roster of enemies during the Second World War.)

During this summer of 1952, I made numerous cross-country flights – as far as Bristol and the Isle of Wight – in a Miles Messenger flown by the amiable Mr. Varcoe, someone high up in Shell Oil's aviation department who hangared his little three-finned monoplane G-AKKG, at White Waltham. (Mr. Varcoe learned to fly in 1917, with the Royal Flying Corps he told me, at Port Meadow, Oxford.) These map-reading exercises, which amounted to fifteen flying hours in all, took me – a sort of "junior spaceman" – to Luton and Cambridge among other places and may have prevented me from getting lost on subsequent solo flights. (Of course, once arrived at my destination, I would have to bring that awkward plane, the Moth, down in one piece.)

At that time, the West London Aero Club operated several pre-war DH 87 Hornet Moth "cabin tourer" biplanes with side-by-side seating. After I got my license, I took my sister up in one of these delightful machines (G-ADNB, built 1936). Of that flight, my sister recalled, "You insisted that I go up flying. The aeroplane bumped around a lot in the air, and I felt queasy. When we got down, I had oil on my dress. Then you wanted me to pay for the flight! To top it all, you put me on the bus home while you stayed at the aerodrome!" I took my brother flying, too. He recalled, "You flew really low over Windsor Castle. It wouldn't be allowed anymore."

Ch. 4. One of the Montreal-built Harvards delivered to the RAF in 1943 and 1944 (photographed at Moreton-in-Marsh, 1954). Engine was the P & W Wasp 1340 cu in. 9 cyl. radial. A lot of them were "pranged" –"flew into a railway tunnel," "hit tree while low flying," etc.

4

THRILLS AND SPILLS

Bye-bye Browning! Bye-bye Keats! When I got the letter from the Air Ministry accepting me for flight training and a short-service commission, I quit school and the Oxbridge track to join the glamorous R.A.F. The first twelve weeks at Kirton-in-Lindsey we were chased from pillar to post on the parade ground, in the barracks, on the firing range, and in the classroom. An exemplary activity was close-order drill with fixed bayonets, when we officer cadets (our blue uniforms set off by white hat bands, white belts and gorget patches) wheeled across the parade ground in tight phalanxes with fierce sergeants snapping at our heels like terriers. My flight commander was Flt. Lt. "Ginger" Lacey, the Battle of Britain ace ("18 E.A. destroyed, and Lacey himself was shot down nine times"). He looked old! He was 36.

This fast pace slowed noticeably when we were posted to flying school, to an aerodrome nominally located at Moreton-in-Marsh, a town near Oxford, but more usefully described as situated beneath a seemingly permanent layer of clouds. Here we got to fly, half days (the other half was ground school), among the noisy little Prentice training planes that swarmed uncertainly around the aerodrome or darted hither and thither on local flights. When we singly and individually were given charge of one or other of these airplanes, we shook loose from the earth to skid around the sky and discover that the world is in reality ninety percent blue-and-white and only ten percent brown-and-green, and that the inhabitants of the British Isles are closed off from the sun for much of their lives by nothing more than an insubstantial cloud layer, easily penetrated. Drugged with this insight, we found our way back to earth, climbed out of our flying machines, and tacked back to the flight office like drunken sailors, the balancing fluid still sloshing around in the semicircular canals of the inner ear.

After seventy hours flying the Percival Prentice primary trainer, I moved up to the North American Harvard (RAF version of the Texan), advanced trainer of 1940 (this was now 1954), which I soloed after 7 1/2 hrs instruction from F/Sgt McFarland. Background: the RAF had a lot of advanced jet fighters and bombers, Hunters, Canberras, Victors, Valiants...but some flying schools got left behind, and Moreton had old airplanes and old pilots. At this time, the early 1950s, the RAF still had five hundred lend-lease Harvard trainers left over from the war, of which one quarter, according to some statistics I read – or misread – were lost in accidents and to sheer exuberance. (FT 376 hit tree while low flying; FT415 flew into railway tunnel; KF140 abandoned out of fuel; KF138 crashed in sea 12 mls. N of Kings Lynn; FX444 hit wind sock on take-off; FS892 crashed on city street in Ely next to the cathedral; and so on. See John F. Hamlin, *The Harvard File*, for details.)

My unit, No. 1 FTS, lost six Harvards while I was there, including one that broke up in a dive 25.8.54, 4 mls. WNW of Stow-on-the-Wold; another when an instructor and student spun into the ground; yet another "cr. Broadway, Worcs, 31.8.54", and so on. In addition, numerous aircraft were damaged in runway accidents. I don't know what the fatality rate was. But the act of flying was expected to be dangerous. An oft-quoted fact is that the R.A.F. and its predecessor the Royal Flying Corps lost more pilots (8,000) in training accidents during WW1 than in combat flying overseas (6,000 fatalities). This was small potatoes compared with WW2, though the percentage of flying accidents (in WW2) might have been lower because more was known about structures, and engines were more reliable – though the weather wasn't. But as for scheduled thrills and spills in 1954, better have gone to see our kindred spirits, the "wall of death" motorbike riders on the Skegness waterfront.

The Harvard was an advanced design for its own time, the mid-1930s, and was not withdrawn from service until early 1955, more than a decade after the RAF entered the jet age, so I was just in time to fly this sporting airplane. At the front end was a big, very noisy, nine-cylinder radial engine which, on take-off and landing, effectively hid the runway from the pilot's view. (The instructor, when aboard, was squirreled away in the rear cockpit.) At the tail end of this airplane was a little wheel with a mind of its own, which helped make the Harvard a frisky airplane indeed. Lined up on the runway for take-off, the pilot must open the throttle smoothly (or the engine would backfire) and barrel down the runway to pick up flying speed. The airplane wanted to swing to the left (from the gyroscopic force of the propeller), and the pilot corrected this with right rudder – but overcorrecting risked a swerve off the runway. Similarly, the approach and landing phase had to be flown carefully. On the third bounce, you needed to "go around again" or the plane would get away from you completely. I saw a few of these runway accidents – not fatal, just a write-off for the airplane involved. So there was the Harvard, smelly, noisy, and often intractable. I liked it. It made a noise like a big motor bike without a muffler; a rasping or howling noise generated by the tips of the propeller exceeding the speed of sound. It is possible that it was the noise level that led me to remember the Harvard over all other airplanes.

A fly in the ointment: after 60 hours with McFarland, I was reassigned to F/ Sgt "Bluebottle" (the nick-name came from a character popular on BBC radio at the time). I confess to an affinity for the straightforward Scots, who had pretty much staffed my boarding school; but I wasn't consulted, and Mac was rotated with the quietly angry Bluebottle who didn't care for me one little bit. He was a Flight Sergeant who aspired to own a grocery store. After the war, after the VE parties, I surmised, life went flat. You were supposed to go home to your wife and dog. And if you couldn't think of anything to do, you stayed in the Air Force, a small cog in a big wheel, and buzzed around the sky disgruntled, up and down the cloud streets and over the abandoned airfields. (Bluebottle: difficult problem, his. How on earth or in the sky does one occupy a whole lifetime? Have to see Plato on that one.)

There were three sets in the RAF: war veterans, National Service inductees (all males eighteen and over had to serve two years in one of the armed services), and postwar volunteers. As for me, I was rethinking the eight years I'd signed on for. My pal Gordon Catto had committed only for the minimum two years, but he was a graduate of Aberdeen University.

Meanwhile there was cross-country training. We navigated by dead reckoning, supplemented by "fixes" obtained from calling any two direction-finding stations and plotting the resultant intersection of position lines on our half-million chart (cumbersome, to say the least). Sometimes the flights were made above the clouds, and the track over the ground only approximated the intended flight path. I might deduce I was over Nottingham, say, when I was actually miles away, over the Spotted Cow public house at Much Snoring. On night cross-countries, they refrained from sending us among the clouds, but even so Gordon Catto, overdue on a clear night, would admit he'd gone twice the distance because "I dropped my pencil and couldn't work out where I was."

At about this time I contracted an ear infection from my head phone. Time dragged while I was sent to Halton hospital for diagnosis and treatment, then waited around to join the next available flying course. The weather didn't help move things along, either: "eleven stationary fronts over the British Isles" was a not an unusual forecast. I went up to London a few times to the theatre district (saw Valerie Hobson, Peter Ustinov, and that crew), took some leave-time hill walking in the Black Coolins of the Isle of Skye, visited the vintage aeroplane collection at Old Warden, Beds., and otherwise passed the time. I'd spent over six months on the ground. I was bored. I thought I'd go to Blackpool to ride the rollercoasters. Then I got on the last Harvard course at Moreton-in-Marsh (before the airplanes were sold as surplus or sent to the scrap heap), and ....I got to fly again. From my notes at the time: "I found a small gap in the clouds at five thousand feet. The clouds were only five hundred feet thick, and it was entirely blue above. I did slow rolls and stall turns above the clouds and out of sight of the ground for about forty minutes."

Airborne in the early morning, I would see fog following the course of the River Severn; at the end of the day, flying into the dazzling sun, long shadows were to be seen to the east of every hill and line of trees, and then, passing over the aerodrome, turning and descending through the scattered white clouds, the pale-green airfield. Solo night cross-country flights stick in my memory, when, after an hour and forty-five minutes of flight, the home base beacon swam into sight flashing the code letters in red, MO MO... Formation flying was the most exhilarating of the exercises, whether flying dual or solo. E Flight's aircraft assembled on the main runway in vee formation. At the signal, all engines opened up. Oh, thunderous, gorgeous noise! Our airplanes, six or nine of them in vics of three, rolling forward, lifting into the air, the student pilots wrestling to keep close but fearing to collide with their consorts. Returning triumphantly to the aerodrome in echelon formation, we awaited the order to break formation and land. Breaking, breaking, NOW, screeched Bluebottle. We were the lead aircraft. I touched down and barreled along the runway, barely stopping at the far boundary.

The Harvard became progressively manageable. Blind take-offs "under the hood" for example, were accomplished by unwavering focus on the direction gyro, while feeding in enough rudder to counter propeller torque. But the pesky Bluebottle was still a buzzing nuisance, and despite McFarland's favorable report, he played his trump card, and I was suspended from the course after 201 hours and 55 mins. "for descending below minimums." This was news to me, as the week before I had passed my instrument rating check. ("I certify I have checked this log book in accordance with AMO 156/54 for issue of white card instrument rating. R.H. Jones, Flt. Lt., IRE.").

"Just think of it as an episode," the wing commander said. "Your National Service requirement is about up." (Bye, bye, Bluebottle! Hello, World!)

5

JOY RIDER

An acquaintance was looking for a partner to fly to New Zealand in an Auster airplane. Did I want to come? Yes. Could I share expenses? No. I had to get paid for doing something. I needed a commercial pilot's license – a lot of expense in those days. (I went up to Leadenhall Street and signed on with the P&O for a voyage to Australia, then another. That's how I paid for my flight training.) I got my flying time at Denham Aerodrome in the Auster Autocrat and the Miles Magister aircraft. I flew some additional hours, concurrently, at Elstree and Croydon; and in between took horseback riding lessons at Pinewood. (I relied on the Thames Valley bus system for my transport.)

One of the requirements for a commercial ticket was a 300 nautical-mile cross country, and I flew this from Denham, in a radio-less Autocrat, landing at Coventry and Exeter, and returning to Denham. Navigation was by map and compass only. I lost time on the first leg, nosing around over the cluttered landscape of the English midlands, squinting at the railway junctions, finally recognizing the bombed-out cathedral at Coventry; and lost time during the second leg to Exeter, too; so I had to make up the time on the third leg, scurrying across Salisbury Plain while sunset blossomed and faded in a pulse of color. Another sunset I remember: while waiting for night flying practice at Croydon, parked next to a yellow-and-silver Hornet Moth of the London Aeroplane Club, I watched hares on the field, and the aircraft landing into the southwest wind, the pilots of those red-washed airplanes peering into the splendour of day's ending. Dusk came; a Tiger Moth taxied in, onto the concrete apron, sending a stream of sparks from its tail skid. That month I took the commercial flying test, and the night cross-country test, in yet another taildragger, the D.H. Chipmunk.

In August 1956 my commercial pilot's license was issued, and I got a job (through a contact made at Croydon) joy-riding on the Norfolk coast starting August 29, although this was late in the season. A man named Wright had rented a 20-acre field at North Denes, where he kept three Auster aircraft (Mk. V war-surplus artillery spotters) during the summer months to fly holiday-makers over the sea front at Gt. Yarmouth and over the basking seals at Scroby Island. I interpreted my job as jumping the Auster over every pier and jetty along the sea front, rushing low over the sea, then banking toward the shore and zooming over the cliffs to the airfield, just beyond the ragged line of trees. Average flight time was fifteen minutes, so it was like working on a Chinese assembly line.

This part of Norfolk is very flat, crossed with drainage cuts. In the River Yare were spritsail barges, the red-painted SHIPWASH lightship, foreign coasters, schooners, and the odd collier. The innumerable white sails of pleasure boats dotted the green expanse of the Broads, and I would fly the length of Breydon Water below the mast height of the sailboats. On two occasions I took an airplane over to Boston for servicing, on the far side of the Wash, looking for the inconspicuous flying field, then landing on what looked like an obstacle course piled with mounds of hay.

September 15 was "Battle of Britain Day", and our three aircraft went to RAF Horsham St Faith to fly joyriders. I arrived first, flying low in front of the control tower, making a very tight one-eighty descending turn to a landing. After thirty-eight joy flights I took off for home. It was a straight hop, taking off and landing into the east wind. I roared low over South Carlton's churches, and saw North Denes aerodrome framed by a big northbound oil tanker. On September 24 I ran the Auster into a boundary fence at the end of the landing run. The summer season was over anyway, and with no airplane I was out of a job. This fast-paced episode fizzled out like a shooting star.

6

HINDOO HOLIDAY

What next? I replied to a "Flight Crew Vacancies" ad in the magazine *Flight* for a helicopter pilot on the Antarctic whaling fleet, presuming that they would supply the rating (what presumption!); and they asked me to send my log book to their London offices, which I did. (Nothing came of it.) Meanwhile, an acquaintance of mine suggested that I apply to a tea company in the City of London, on Mincing Lane, and I went there one fine day in the autumn of 1956 to interview for a job in Assam. The company wanted a trainee tea planter who could also fly the company plane (or was it the other way around?) There were two interviews: one by a planter who had been a Fleet Air Arm pilot in Korea, flying the Hawker Sea Fury (he drank a lot of gin he said, of his war-time flying); the other, with a genial old planter, a company director, who had been an under-gardener at Kew, switched to tea planting, and spent forty years in Assam before retiring to the head office. Getting ahead of the story – there wasn't nearly enough flying to offset the disadvantages of staying on an isolated plantation in Assam. The starting pay was low, the management aloof and censorious, the Indian bureaucracy obstructive. Sifting through the whole experience, it is the sight of the Himalayas that justifies the time spent on this gig: those remote peaks that hovered in the upper reaches of the air, far above the heat, garish colors, pungent smells, and abject poverty of India.

Early in January 1957, I went by British Overseas Airways, by Canadair prop plane, to Calcutta, and contacted the agents about a passage up country. I went to the not very grand Grand Hotel, on Chowringhee Street, stepping over people sleeping in the street and in the Maidan Park. I stayed in this hotel for a few days, fending off the mosquitoes, while making arrangements to go up country. Also staying there were the Dalai and Panchen Lamas of Tibet, with their entourage of shaven-headed, saffron-robed monks carrying prayer wheels. The Dalai Lama was exactly my age. (But then – Great Balls of Fire – so was Jerry Lee Lewis and Elvis Presley, to mention only two other leading spirits of the age.)

I went to Dum Dum airport and looked for the Assam plane, and I found a place for myself among the empty tea chests before the Dakota took off and climbed high over the Naga Hills. (I was wearing khaki shorts, so I was cold.) The Brahmaputra Valley in Assam is about three hundred fifty miles long, and dead-ends into the "hump" of Himalayan China. At this time, in the 1950s, the English tea companies had about fifty airstrips along this valley, on both sides of the river, and several of the companies and a few individual planters operated light airplanes, mostly Austers, to get around more quickly than was possible by car. Why so air-minded? Possibly because during the war, this was the site of the massive American airlift from Assam over the hump to Kunming, China, and several of the wartime airports remained, including Tezpur – my destination this morning. After the war, tea was airlifted to Calcutta instead of going by train.

When the plane landed, I was met by a Sikh, a tea-factory assistant, he explained, who drove me to the Majulighur Tea Garden. There I met Tony Torrance, with whom I was initially to share a bungalow. Tony, who had been out about five years, was ten years my senior, ex RAF and Bristol University, "a bit of a character." He drove a Model T Ford with a thatched roof. He took me to see the manager of the tea company, and later to meet the super-intendent who overlorded three such gardens. "His name is Hannay, as in *Thirty-nine Steps* [the thriller by John Buchan]. Drinks like a fish and thinks he knows everything." Each of the three gardens, Tony explained, was about one thousand acres in extent, and each garden employed a thousand workers or more. The English managers' bungalows were dispersed, each on a separate section of the tea garden, presumably in the interests of better supervision. Tony's bungalow was typically spacious, and manned by a dozen servants. Among them: two bearers (butlers), each on an eight-hour shift; and a night watchman *(chowkidar)*, who padded around silently in his bare feet skewering giant cockroaches with his broad-bladed spear. In addition, there was a cook (his kitchen was housed in a separate building); a water carrier *(pani wallah)*; a groom *(syce)*; two gardeners (one, walking without a lantern, had been eaten by a tiger); and – lowest in caste – a sweeper. At breakfast, on the lawn of the bungalow, I could clearly see Mt. Kangto, 23,260 feet high – and never climbed – about eighty miles to the north, on the border with Tibet. How's that for a view while you eat the breakfast egg! (All this territory – everything 25 miles north of us, in fact, the old North East Frontier Agency – was currently claimed by the Red Chinese. In 1962, they invaded as far as Tezpur. I never checked on what happened to the tea planters.

The Majuli Tea Company operated a single Auster Aiglet, a four-seater with a 130 HP de Havilland engine and no electric starter. She was due for an annual inspection in Calcutta, but before then Tony took me on familiarization flights into some twenty landing fields, mostly on tea gardens. We also went on an overnight camping trip into the forest north of the tea plantations, and made a two-day visit to the Kaziranga Reserve, riding around on elephants to see the rhinos there. (Tony, who subsequently went back to London to work as a stockbroker, was obviously proud of his Indian domain.)

Our flight to Calcutta necessitated a dogleg around East Pakistan, a 630-mile flight, more than fifty percent longer than the direct route. First we flew west for two hours, the seasonal east wind pushing us along. The foothills of the Himalayas were always to the right. There was a lone tea garden against Bhutan. It had a name on the roof. I took up the binoculars and read JAINTI – so I could figure our ground speed was constant at 130 mph. We climbed above haze to see Mount Kanchenjunga (28,169 ft), and I sketched the profile of the great mountain in my notebook. Everest was in cloud, and we descended to land at Katihar for petrol. This was very near to the base from which the 1933 Houston-Westland expedition overflew Everest in an open-cockpit biplane. (There is a wonderful illustrated book on this expedition by pilots Clydesdale and McIntyre.) Lady Houston, who financed the expedition, was a millionaire and former showgirl who got caught up in this impulse of the British to rise to the apogee. (Everest would be climbed in 1952.) From Katihar, we flew through the narrow corridor between Nepal and East Pakistan, and then over the Ganges – the sandy banks must have been a mile wide, in this, the dry season – and on through the haze to pinpoint Katwa. The constant growl of the engine and rush of the slip stream inhibited talking. Arrived Dum Dum Airport, 2.05P; Marshal Zhukov's TU-104, with hammer and sickle on the tail, was on the tarmac.

After we got back to Majulighur, the Assam Post Office went on strike, or threatened to strike. I was told by the manager to go to Borengajuli near the SE corner of Bhutan, borrow a plane (an Auster Mk V) from a planter, and fly east as far as Bordubi, which is near Sookerating, to carry company mail. That's 260 miles, almost to the Hump itself, the length of the upper Brahmaputra Valley. I don't remember how I got to Borengajuli, probably in someone's car. (I got around Majulighur by bike or on horseback.) The planter told me that the Auster's Lycoming engine was due for an overhaul, and that the spark plugs oiled up and needed to be removed and cleaned at every stop. He told me that avgas was lacking at several of my planned stops, so I picked up two five-gallon cans of fuel at an estate named Behora, south of the river. Anyway, I was happy to be let loose over Assam.

They weren't expecting me at Bordubi, my farthest stop, but gave me lunch, and after I cleaned the plugs I headed back to Gotoonga. Seventy-five minutes later, I was wondering where I was. Oil on the windscreen obscured vision ahead, and the gathering dusk permitted only a few miles visibility. Well, I was somewhere on the Bengal and Assam Railway – whose tracks I had been following. I flew a little further down the track until the latest time I thought I must turn north (I kept looking at my watch). Then I turned north and looked for Gotoonga on the left – surely I hadn't passed it? – and then, hey presto, it was there on the right – I hadn't overshot the place – and I landed at 5.32P, before dark.

The next day I backtracked NE to a place named Thowra, where I was supposed to pick up a Mr. Liddle at noon, and fly him to Jorhat (another former American air base) to connect with the plane to Calcutta and thence to London. After almost an hour waiting at the Thowra airstrip, I left the plane and went to find the manager of this estate. I found him in his bungalow, hosting a party. Mr. Johnson? A man who looked like a film star (odd, that) came forward and invited me to join his guests. I took a drink; explained that I was looking for a Mr. Liddle. He knew nothing of him. Within ten minutes a jeep drew up; my passenger was at the airfield. I rushed off amid good-byes and laughter. "You'll miss your connection!" "No. It's standard time the airlines work on." I took off, and when the compass settled down, I picked up the trunk road to Jorhat. I shouldn't have been going into this main-line airport because I didn't have an Indian flying license yet – didn't get one until the end of May, when I went to Delhi. (I was able to make a side trip to Agra, by myself, by train, in order to see the Taj Mahal by moonlight. The chowkidars were asleep, and I had to force a side door before I could rouse them.)

April 29: Tony was to catch the 4.00P plane from Tezpur to Calcutta and thence to London. I was at our airstrip, waiting for him in the Auster. Tony drove up late and threw three *maunds* of baggage (about 250 lbs) into the back of the plane. We took off, and before we reached Tezpur the Calcutta plane, a DC3, overhauled us from the east. Tony mentioned he couldn't find his ticket. We landed right behind the DC3, and Tony went to check in while I unloaded the Aiglet as fast as I could – the temperature was about one hundred degrees – watched by a score of passengers and loafers. After Tony left, I set the throttle and switches, and swung the propeller by hand. She started with a roar, and – disregarding the brakes – started to roll forward. I jumped in, quick. (That was not the last I saw of Tony. After he went back to England, I visited him at his country house in Essex.)

Back at the tea garden, the day started with *kamjari*, the day's work program, as ordered by the manager or superintendant. If young tea plants were to be watered I would go down to a stream with a gang of women, and they would fill their pitchers, balance them on their heads, and follow me in a long line back to the plantings. But sometimes they wanted to collect firewood for their own account, for which I admonished them, thereby causing an incident. And I took my turn to preside at pay parade. The *babu* (clerk) would read the worker's name and amount of pay due, I would count out the rupees and hand them to the *sirdhar* (foreman). When an untouchable came for his pay, the sirdhar would toss the money on the ground, as custom forbids direct contact. (Queer place, this.)

In fact, I received little or no guidance in dealing with the labour, or in any other aspect of tea planting, either from the manager or the superintendent. The matter of the firewood still festered with them. Finally it dawned on me that London had hired me without properly consulting the superintendent, "39 Steps" – and that this arrangement was a non-starter. What was I doing here anyway? Obviously I was chasing the chimera of flight, but I expected to have some sport doing it, and that wasn't happening. So I left Assam at the time of the monsoon. As the great Tibetan plateau heats up and becomes a low pressure area, the central Asian wind system reverses direction and brings the southwest monsoon. June 1957: the winds at Majulighur were light and variable, the temperature went to one hundred – and the rains were late. At first the northern limit of the monsoon air extended only across the southern end of the Indian peninsula. Then a weak current entered Assam, bringing thunderstorms to the northeast. But Bengal and the populous Indo-Gangetic plain were left wishing.

On the overcast morning of 18 June, the Dakota lined up for takeoff, facing west. The prevailing wind had finally changed. We were soon over Majulighur again, the name in large letters on the roof of a tea-drying house. Some small distance away, flanked by Flame of the Forest trees, was the bungalow I had left that morning. There were thatched huts in their compounds. There was a peasant in a big, round cooli hat, his bullock leaving a wake as it crossed a flooded rice field. The weather closed in. Steaming rain fell from the nimbo-stratus whose black undersides lay not much above the tree tops and enveloped the isolated hilltops. Between earth and clouds, the Dakota banked continuously, flying a twisting course to avoid the darker, more ominous storm clouds. Then the rain ceased. We left the dark country of Assam behind and flew across the dreary yellows and browns of Bengal.

After reflecting on my various flying experiences – with Bluebottle, 15-minute joy hops, and "39 steps" – I decided I would buzz around the sky on my own terms, but in no event in someone's employ.

Within two months I was on the boat from Southampton bound for the New World.

Author's note: Hindoo Holiday: An Indian Journal (1932) is a comic memoir written by J. R. Ackeley.

Ch. 7. Ron Harrison (center), my mother's younger brother, my boyhood hero, trained in Canada, qualified above-average on Spitfires; his airplane was shot-up by ground fire in the Battle of Dieppe, 8/19/1942. He crashed into a mountain on patrol over Wales, 10/21/1942, with two other Spits. "The crows pecked out their eyes," the shepherd who found them reported apologetically. (The gods had exacted a cruel price for the gift of flight.)

7

CANADA

"Y'should have come in the spring of the year," I was told when I arrived in Toronto. "Things pretty much close down in the winter." I'd never thought of that. (Never mind. Something would turn up.)

The only thing I knew about Canada was Ron's photo album. In the spring of 1941 my uncles Ron and John (who lived around the corner from us in Slough), rode their motorbikes to Newbury, to "join up." John enlisted in the army (he would campaign with the 11th Armored Division from Normandy to the Baltic, liberating Belsen Concentration Camp on the way – "the stink was indescribable," he told us years later). Ron, who had always wanted to fly, was accepted in the Royal Air Force Volunteer Reserve.

(Where was my father? Entombed in the Khedival mail steamer *Abukir*, fifty miles off the English coast in seventeen fathoms of water. She is still there, seventy years later. One of the catalogue of a thousand ships (a Homeric number) that rescued most of the BEF from the shoal coast of the channel ports in May 1940, her end was recorded in a small masterpiece of reporting, now in the Public Record Office, by her second officer, Mr. V. P. Wills-Rust.)

Buoyed by the prospect of flight, Ron quit his job as a draftsman and, with no seer to warn him, headed to Canada for flight training. Glamorous Canada: a mix of modernity, wide-open spaces, and "Mounties" – the image so successfully promoted by the Canadian Pacific Railway in the 1930s. Ron traveled by ship to Halifax and continued on by train for two thousand miles to Medicine Hat, Alberta. (This at the very time a large crew from Hollywood was making the "recruiting poster" film, *Captains of the Clouds*, at a place I would come to know – Trout Lake, Ontario.) After a flying course of nineteen weeks on the Tiger Moth and Harvard airplanes, he returned to England by convoy in January 1942, a very active time for U-boats. He completed flight training in England and qualified "Above Average" on Spitfires. He was posted to No.41 Squadron. My mother told me, "Ron had his hair cut very short. He looked like a Hun!" (This was an anomaly, as RAF pilots were popularly known as "Brylcream Boys.")

Ron's first big "op" was on August 19, 1942, the day the Canadian Army mounted the disastrous large-scale raid on Dieppe. Sixty-seven RAF squadrons flew in support of this operation. No. 41 was assigned to escort ground-attack Hurricanes. This was claimed as the greatest single air battle of the war in terms of aircraft lost – over one hundred fifty in sixteen hours. His CO, Squadron Leader Hyde, was shot down, killed, in the diving attack on gun emplacements, and five of the squadron's Spitfires were damaged. Ron's plane was hit, and the engine revs stuck at 2200 RPM. He flew the hundred miles back across the channel to Tangmere, shut off his engine, and made a "dead stick landing" – no easy maneuver for a high-performance airplane landing on a small grass airfield.

Later that summer, 41 Sqn. was deployed to Llanbedr in North Wales. On October 21, Ron was killed when his Spitfire, in formation with two others on coast patrol, crashed full tilt into a Welsh mountain. They crashed near the top of the rounded, grass-covered terrain, leaving the mangled, decapitated bodies of the pilots and the wreckage of the three airplanes. (Was the flight leader disoriented? Why didn't he fly two minutes west and let down over the sea? Was there no ground radar? No-one said.) The site was described to my brother, thirty years later, when he searched out Mr. Williams, the shepherd who found the crash. "The crows pecked out their eyes," he said, as if in apology. So the three flyers suffered the same fate as Homeric heroes slain in battle.

There are no mountains on the sunlit prairies, poor preparation for flying in Wales. There is only sunlight. And does not sunlight promote a sunny outlook? I push this connection on the slender evidence of a short visit to Saskatoon. From a cheerful restaurant there (the waitress was telling, cheerfully, how her brother lost his car in a poker game), I chanced to call at the agricultural museum. The curator, cheerful George Shepherd, recalled that he, with his family, settled here in 1908, out on the prairie, at a place marked by surveyor stakes. His mother brought the family piano from England. "Everyone was so cheerful," he told me. (Optimism: the essential story of the New World.)

It was in 1958 that I lost my way the very first time that I flew over the Canadian forest – symbolic of my ongoing career search? It happened this way. One spring day Al Lavinski and I rented a sixty-five-horsepower Fleet Canuck from Toronto's Island airport to fly a roundabout route to Muskoka. In the course of this flight the wind backed and blew us thirty degrees off course, eastward over Algonquin National Park. I was unaware of this; I only knew that we were overdue our ETA. We were lost. There were no useful landmarks. Other than the countless lakes, there was only the occasional sawmill in the thick forest; nothing to see but clouds, trees and water. We were lost, but we were having a good time away from Toronto. Eventually we came on a railway track in the forest and followed it west. We were seventy six minutes past our ETA Muskoka. Funny, I spent a year in Canada, and only this day stands out in my memory. That, and a short, precarious canoe trip on Lake Ontario.

By the time spring came around and I had the smell of a job at the Island Airport, I had arranged to move to Chicago. (I eventually did quite a bit of sport flying in Canada. It's a great place.)

8

FLYING THE "AIR KNOCKER"

Everything opened up for me when I went to Chicago in the fall of 1958. (I had been invited to visit by a fellow passenger on the westward-bound SS *United States* the year before, Maggie Pond, a student returning from a first visit to Europe.) Chicago: A dynamo of a place. Railways going every which way, sky-scrapers with cavernous lobbies, saloon bars open from 6.00A. In no time I got a starter job in a bank, working nights on La Salle Street; in no time I enrolled in a full-time college program during the day. (I had set myself up to run short on sleep.)

It was incidental that I saw the busiest airport in the world. Squeezed on to 640 acres, Midway handled 431,000 flights a year and ten million passengers. My recollection is of the overwhelming sight and sound of whirring silver propellers; the silhouettes of the curvaceous, three-finned Lockheed Constellations at the ramp, and the heart-thumping effect of encountering scores of nubile stewardesses hurrying through the terminal.

Fifteen miles away, on Roosevelt Road, was York Township airfield, one of many suburban airfields, a hardscrabble place of eighty acres, with two gravel runways that played hell with propellers, and some ramshackle hangars. (Many of the resident airplanes were "tie-downs.") And here was to be found the "Air Knocker". Properly known as the Aeronca Champion, this paragon of buoyancy was a fabric-covered taildragger with a high wing, fat belly, and puny engine. Aeronca produced ten thousand such aircraft between 1945 and 1951 in a plant near Dayton, Ohio. They sold for under $2,000 new, and competed in the light airplane market with the Piper Cub, a skinny, yellow-painted bird, altogether more awkward to handle than the Champ.

I don't know how the Champ came by its unflattering nickname Air Knocker (but its predecessor, the Aeronca C-2, was known as the Flying Bathtub). It was a case of "sticks and stones will break my bones..." The Champ was king of the air in this suburb, could soar over the traffic jam and turn up its snub nose at the roads which channeled and funneled all the road traffic into ... more congestion. York Airport was a short bicycle ride from my friends' place in Glen Ellyn, and – happy days – the Champ rented for $5 an hour, "wet".

The airport was owned and operated by two brothers, Herb and Emile Miller. Herb was the pilot-instructor; Emile, the mechanic. I never heard Emile say anything, at least not to me, and Herb was laconic at best. They had started the airport in 1929 with an OX-5-engined airplane for instruction. "It leaked plenty," said Herb of the water-cooled engine, "and soaked the ignition wires, and the engine would quit and we'd go down in a field." They survived the depression; if they didn't talk much, they didn't miss anything, either. They saw the world through horse traders' eyes, and they knew the value of a dollar. Herb could be affable when he wanted, but more often he could be cantankerous. I have seen him refuse to sell gas to an itinerant pilot, to turn him away because he, Herb, felt he didn't get enough respect or got the wrong vibes from the intruder. I noticed that the Miller brothers didn't work much, mostly polished the seats of their chairs. Emile had an assistant who did the messy work. Herb flew only when he felt like it.

6/19/1959. Herb soloed me in the Champ after two hours instruction.

8/26/1959. We flew cross-country to Starved Rock State Park, about sixty miles southwest on the Illinois River. The view for both occupants of the tandem-seat Champ was spectacular. The little Champ sailed into the air, over the houses, over the roads and the fields, and landed on the island in the river beside Starved Rock, a tall sandstone butte. Here, in an incident in the French and Indian War, a band of Illini Indians were said to have been trapped and starved out by the Ottawas. The explorer La Salle came to Starved Rock, too, in a canoe from Montreal. He convinced himself he was on his way to China, but had taken the same wrong turn as Louis Joliet and was on his way to the Gulf of Mexico.

I recall this time as a sort of aeronautical Arcadia. I got my private pilot license here at York in 1960 and celebrated on Columbus Day, a gorgeous fall day, by making a 4hr 45 min flight over Wisconsin's farms and little towns. I took along a friend, Ian Suter, who was visiting from England. I wonder if he remembers that day? Other days I flew the Champ solo around Lake Michigan's shore to Benton Harbor, and to Mount Hawley airfield in Peoria.

After Helen and I married, she soloed the same Champ, and we bought a Cessna 180 from Herb in April 1967 (this airplane caused me some grief, I'll allow) and kept it hangared at York until the airport closed in Nov. 1968.

Meanwhile I could rent a four-place Cherokee airplane from nearby Mitchell Field, in Lombard (that was before I got the Cessna 180). By that time I was working for Tom Miner, whose offices were in the penthouse suite of the Field Building at 135 South La Salle Street. (There was a view of Meigs Field.) One of our clients – Bandag, the tire retread manufacturer – was in Muscatine, Iowa. August 1966 I flew down to see Bandag to present a report. It was 150 miles west. When I was in the air I realized I'd put my chart in the baggage compartment. Not to worry! I couldn't miss the Mississippi River, where Bandag was located, and meanwhile I could check my position by reading the names of towns on the ubiquitous municipal water tanks en route. After my visit (I had one colleague as passenger) the president, Mr. Carver, presented us with a giant watermelon, a speciality of the place, and strapped it in the rear seat of the Cherokee for us. That's how things were in the heady days of the 'sixties.

Ch. 9. America as playground: Self on tow in a Schweitzer 1-26, setting out for Pike's Peak (seen in background) to "catch the wave," Dec. 27, 1963. Soaring is the purest form of flying.

9

PIKES PEAK
(AMERICA AS PLAYGROUND)

Was this the briefest and best of my flying experiences? Probably, yes. The Chicago Glider Club, then based at Clow Field, was 30 minutes from Glen Ellyn. They were a friendly lot, mostly airline pilots. I was soloed after two hours of air tows in a Schleicher K7, had an FAA check ride on site, and was soon riding the thermals. WHOOSH! From fourteen hundred feet to fifty-two hundred on one thermal! The energy of the thermals was palpable. Then, after an hour's free flight, I looked for the landing site. Where was it? I was losing height all the time. There, I saw it! Over there! On the other side of the plane! But I got in O.K. Whew! After seven hours gliding, taking up friends as passengers and so forth, Dale May offered me a ride out to Colorado Springs, to Black Forest Glider Port, in his Cessna 180 to try out the soaring. Our flight of one thousand miles into wind took eight hours, with stops in Iowa and Kansas. Pikes Peak was visible 130 miles out.

The day after we arrived, December 27, 1963, the weather was perfect for soaring. With the wind from WNW, there would be a lee wave downwind of Pikes Peak. The little Schweitzer sailplane was hooked up to the tow plane. There was the mountain, twenty miles away, looking much nearer. I got into an insulated flying suit, pulled on three pairs of socks, then fleece-lined boots. I took hold of parachute and oxygen mask. "If you have to come down," they said, pointing at a map, "there's a golf course, a race track, and a ranch – here." I felt a sharp anticipation, because I hadn't piloted a 1-26 glider before, or flown over a mountain.

It was like the first time on water skis, that air tow: wild oscillations on the end of the tow rope, the glider plunging and yawing and rolling. After fifty minutes – a rough ride – I was positioned in the narrow primary wave and released. I was eight miles downwind of Pikes Peak, level with its summit. Here was smooth flying. I sat there in the wave, balancing on a ball, seeing a hundred miles, soaring ever upwards, listening to the wind, holding my position over the ground by nosing down into the rushing air – but always rising. After two hours, a bank of clouds drove me away from my catbird seat at 18,000 feet, and I glided easily twenty-five miles back to Black Forest airfield, whence I had started.

The following day I flew three winch tows to 1600 feet, but failed to find lift.

(For the next few years, much of my time was taken up traveling to exotic places for my job as well as chasing after girl friend Helen Collins, who was at the University of Michigan and whom I married in !966. (We went on the QM to Cherbourg.) We stayed in the Chicago area until 1975. Those were good years.)

Ch. 10. 1955 Cessna 180 N3372D at Nuevo Casas Grandes, Mexico, 1969. Based at Glen Ellyn, Illinois (York Township Airport) this was our "go anywhere" airplane. The 180 was introduced in 1953. Geraldine Mock, a "housewife from Ohio," flew a 180 around the world in 1964. Engine is a 6 cyl. 470 cu.in. Continental, developing 230 HP. It cost me $24/hour to run this airplane.

10

"MY THREE BIG FLIGHTS"
(CESSNA 180, N3372D)

In those days flying had not lost its novelty, nor price inflation and over-regulation become oppressive. So the world was at my fingertips when I owned a Cessna 180, the best all-round bush plane of its class. The 180 was hangared at Millers' little airport (soon to be sold off for a building lot), a mile and a half from our apartment on Roosevelt Road. She was a good, fast plane, a 1955 model with Goodyear crosswind landing gear, capable of flying out of a farmer's field or going anywhere in this huge playground of North America (or around the world, as Jerrie Mock did in 1964 in her 180). The 180 was a "hot rod" when it came out in 1953, considered by some to be "over-powered"; soon it was in general use around the world. Ernest Hemingway mentions the 180 favorably in his Africa diary.

I flew 3372D for two years, 454 hours in total. Most of these flights were in the Midwest; others to New York, New Orleans, and Texas. One of the first things I did with this long-range airplane was to fly the twenty miles to Meigs Field on Chicago's spectacular waterfront, a short taxi ride from my office. "Flying to work" was a vision of the 1930s from *Life* magazine. It felt great! This is what flying was all about, I thought: complete freedom to go where I wanted.

I recall flying to Brownsville on the Gulf coast, low across the one million acres of the King Ranch and on to San Antonio and Dallas. Coming back from the Texas State Fair, I ran into fog and made a forced landing in a farm field near Bloomington, Illinois. "Where you from?" demanded the surprised farm hand. "Dallas, Texas," I said. I got into the cab of his truck to drive out of there, but his tires just spun in the mud. I was back in Illinois, stuck in the mud, pretty pleased with everything.

My "three big flights" in this airplane (title borrowed from Bleriot XI pilot Andre Beaumont's 1911 book) were:

California	5,000 miles	8/27/67 – 9/9/67
Alaska	7,910 miles	6/2/68 – 6/25/68 *
Mexico	7,585 miles	2/14/69 – 3/15/69 *

abstracts of my articles published by Aero magazine (1970)

Anyone who had the time could do this, I realized, and these flights were only remarkable for their ease of accomplishment and the marvelous vistas en route. (A measure of "progress in flying machines" predicted by Octave Chanute in 1894!) The charts, the gasoline, and the weather reports were all available as a matter of course. In 1967, the FAA published a booklet on "Terrain Flying" for North America, including Mexico, with a lot of notes on specific routes. With that kind of route information, and a wariness for conditions of poor visibility (current knowledge of the spread between the temperature and the dew point) most trips could be safely completed.

Most of the time, America's flying weather is good. Practically, that means if you, the private pilot, can spend the odd day or days waiting out the weather front, you can fly all over North America in a light airplane equipped only for VFR flying. Expensive radios and instruments, which themselves can cost more than a used light airplane, are redundant. If you are a doctor or a lawyer, though, who has to be back in the office for that Monday morning meeting, better park your airplane and fly a commercial airliner. Take your time!

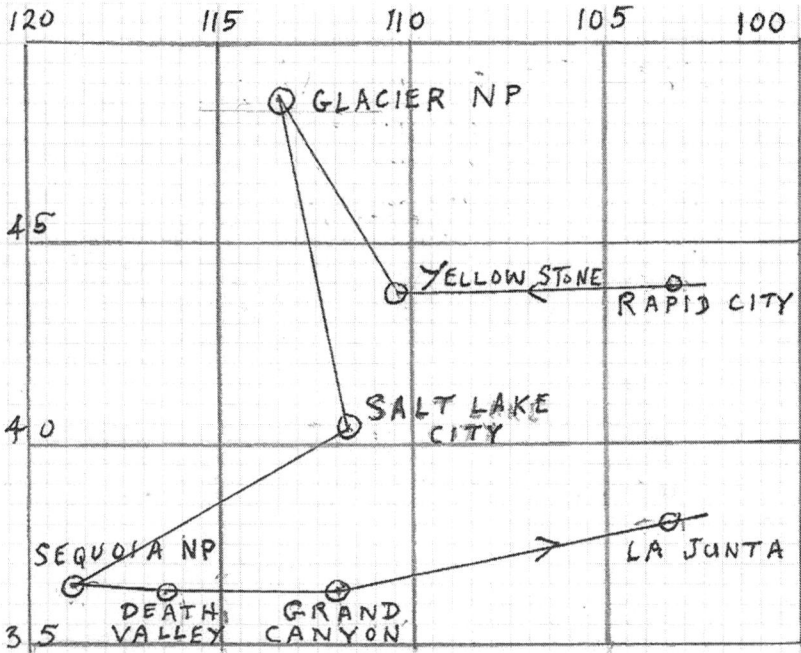

Glen Ellyn to Yellowstone

We waited for a break in the weather; then, a day late, we took off in light rain showers, breaking out from them near the Mississippi River. We re-fueled at Rapid City, SD. Farther on, in the Powder River country, the wide-open spaces became more desolate; and we flew on, dodging late-afternoon thundershowers, and landed at Worland, Wyoming. We had flown beyond 99W into the parched plains of the West.

Next day the morning was sparkling clear. We flew high over Cody towards Yellowstone, at 14,500 feet, sipping oxygen from a tank. The jagged Tetons could be seen miles off to the south. Landed at West Yellowstone, where we pitched our tent near a river and stayed two nights. We watched ospreys curving over the torrent in the Yellowstone Canyon. The second night we were scared out of our tent by a grizzly bear, and took refuge in our rented car.

Yellowstone to Glacier, along the Continental Divide

The route from Yellowstone to Glacier National Park goes NNW, following the high country of the Continental Divide. It took us 2 hr 10 min to get to Glacier Park airport (then named Flathead). We landed there at 12.05P on 30 August, and then moved to nearby Kalispell to spend the night. Our plan was to cross the Park, flying west to east, to get a good look at the terrain. Our first attempt, taking off at 7.55A on the following day, was thwarted by smoke from forest fires, but a second attempt, at 9.45A was successful, and we cruised over knife-edge arêtes and above blue lakes high in the corries.

Glacier to Sequoia

Now we were bound for Sequoia National Park, more than a thousand miles to the southwest, eight or ten easy flying hours, with overnight stops at Helena and Salt Lake City. Our route involved a long stretch over desolate Nevada, and then, rounding the northern edge of the White Mountains (coming into Owens Valley), we caught our first sight of the Sierra Nevada, a long wall of somber mountains capped in grey clouds. We approached cautiously, wondering whether the low (10,000 feet) pass at Mammoth Mountain was clear of clouds. We scraped under the clouds there, and burst into the San Joaquin River valley, making a left turn toward Fresno. There we rented a car and spent three nights on a camping-hiking trip in Sequoia National Park, and saw the John Muir Grove and other giant trees.

Sequoia to Grand Canyon

08.30, September 5. Left Fresno for Death Valley Airport, two hundred miles and two hours away. Once again, light winds minimized turbulence. The crest line of the Sierras is exactly eighty miles east of Fresno, and at 8.30A we climbed toward it, leveling out at 14,500 feet, following Kings Canyon, and landed at Death Valley airport, which is 211 feet below sea level. We stayed there just one-and-a-half hours and flew on to Cedar City, Utah, after a four-hour stop at Las Vegas (got to visit a theater show). We arrived at Grand Canyon the following day, pitched our tents for an over-night stay, and then made a couple of flights exploring the canyon, flying 2,200 feet below the rim. Big country! Small airplane!

Grand Canyon to Glen Ellyn

We left Grand Canyon airport at 3.45P, bound for Montrose, Colorado. A long line of towering thunderstorms blocked our way and kept us flying east, across a huge Indian Reservation, to Gallup, New Mexico, where we spent the night. The next day we flew through the twisting pass at Taos, and dropped into the large, lonely airfield at La Junta. We ate lunch in town, and Helen bought an Indian blanket. Next day we were back home in Glen Ellyn at 3.00P in the afternoon, thus completing a spectacular 5,000-mile trip.

Essence of trip

Power of movement; flying is the ideal way of touring the West – minimizes monotony of plains, highlights the drama of the Sierras and the Grand Canyon.

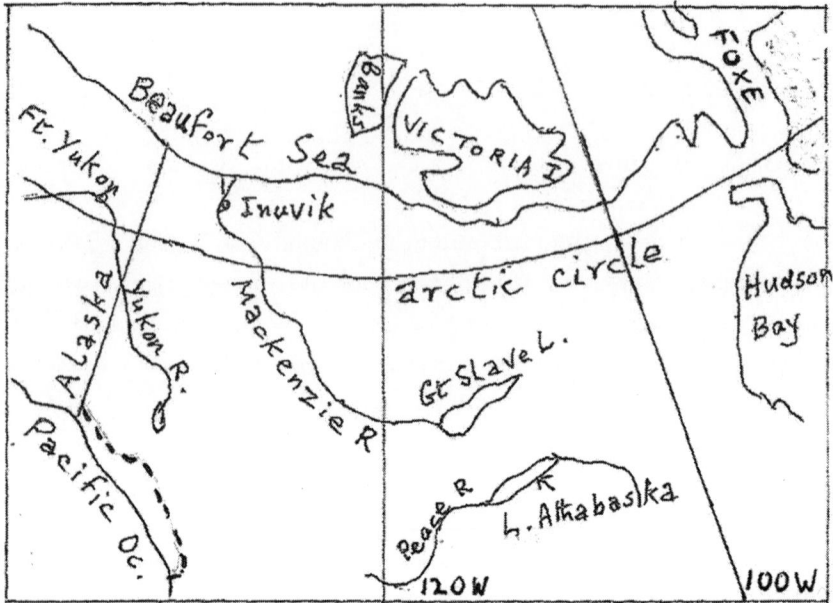

To help with the navigation, I installed a new direction gyro, checked the radios and the ADF, and installed a trailing aerial on the HF radio. Meanwhile, Helen and I listed and packed 143 items ranging from tents, pots, tie-downs, ammo and dried food to first-aid kit. With all our gear, and full tanks, the 180 would be lifting a load of 986 lbs. Before loading and fuelling our airplane, we moved her to the longer runway at West Chicago airport, about ten miles down the road.

To Whitehorse

6/2/1968. West Chicago. Our heavy airplane pushed out into the choppy air, away from the little harbor of the airport, away from its dull hinterlands, on a new voyage. We headed for Flying Cloud Airport, Minneapolis, passing a flight of snow geese en route. I noted little flecks of oil coming back on the windscreen.

At the end of the second day, we completed the 1,500 miles to Banff by landing at its spectacular airfield. Here at Banff, in the Rockies, was our best camp site, and from there we took a side trip by car to Lake Louise. Then, a very scenic flight along the Ice Field Highway to Jasper, flying lower than the snowy peaks on both sides. But oil was still coming back onto the windscreen, though they had put in new propeller seals at both Regina and Calgary. From Jasper, we joined the Alaska Highway at Fort St. John, and followed it along the broad valleys of British Columbia and the Yukon.

Rattling around in my head were the verses of Robert Service, particularly the story of Sam McGee from Tennessee. In this land of gold strikes, Service made his fortune from versifying about the Land of the Midnight Sun.

Farther and farther our trajectory took us, to be swallowed up over the wide open country of British Columbia, a landscape forlorn, turreted with thunder clouds. Heavy showers forced us to dog leg considerably off the Highway near Pink Mountain, B.C., and in doing so we passed low over some very isolated and barely accessible farms.

To McKinley Park

At Whitehorse we decided to detour to Glacier Bay across the mountains and down to the ocean. On the first try, headed for Juneau with a favorable weather report, rain and cloud turned us back. Next day, a second try, departing at 4.20A, didn't work but a third attempt, leaving Whitehorse at 8.20A, was successful and we flew to Juneau in 1hr 40 mins. Visibility on the coast was one hundred miles, and we made a left-hand circuit of Glacier Bay at 6,000 feet. Spotting whales in Icy Strait, we spiraled down to the green waters for a better view. Back in Whitehorse, we passed through customs once again, then pushed on to Northway, a friendly place to stay the night.

6/13/1968. Detouring sixty miles west of McKinley Park Airfield, we saw Mount Denali looming mightily out of proportion. By this time of the morning, the cumulus had built up, and a brief drumming of hail from an overhanging thunderhead dented our control surfaces as we returned to the airfield. Camped in the Park we saw straw-colored grizzly bears, red fox, moose and beaver. Overhead flew mew gulls, jaegers and golden eagles.

To Inuvik

6/15/1968. Fort Yukon, an old Hudson Bay post. At this time of the year, there was sunlight round the clock. It took an effort to go to sleep at night. We made one side trip up to Arctic Village, 110 miles north on the Arctic Circle, at the foot of the Brooks Range. For our next leg, northeast to Inuvik, Cliff Fairchild, who ran the air service at Fort Yukon, gave me a word of caution. When I filed our flight plan with him, he told me there was no weather report available, except, once in the air, by calling ahead to Inuvik. We took off in light rain, intending to test the weather, and flew down the Porcupine River, while the weather gradually improved. This is remote country. Just past the tiny settlement of Old Crow, I unreeled the trailing aerial, and called Inuvik on 3023.5. They reported their weather as "High overcast; visibility more than one-five." Soon our ADF needle homed on the powerful beacon there. Below us a tundra fire was blazing fiercely. Two and a half hours from Fort Yukon, we arrived over the immense pocked delta of the Mackenzie.

To Hudson's Bay

1,077 miles from Inuvik, at the junction of the Peace and the Slave Rivers – easy navigation, following the Mackenzie River – is Wood Buffalo Park, the largest national park in the world. Having rented a car at Fort Smith to see some buffalo, we became mired in the muddy track of a road for some hours, until a ranger rescued us. Without the head nets and gloves we had with us, the biting insects would have driven us crazy.

Churchill is 745 miles east from there. But with no river to follow, I set the gyro carefully to fly across the huge assembly of lakes. The magnetic compass would be of little use once I noticed the variation was 35 degrees with a further unexplained error of 25 degrees. Unfortunately, the radio beacon at Lynn Lake, our intermediate stop, had a range of only forty miles. Anyway, we made it to Churchill by map reading, wary of the precession of the directional gyro.

We reached Churchill on June 19. Hudson Bay was beginning to break up. Churchill is a rundown place, but interesting for all that. We hired some Eskimos to take us to see the beluga whales, which were then arriving from the far north. I searched out some of the few knowledgeable persons in town to ask about the natural history. There are thousands of seals in the vicinity at this time of year, they told us, but no polar bears until September and October. The Bay does not freeze over.

The Fog; The Red Dye Test.

We were to leave Churchill for Chicago on June 21st. Despite the favorable weather report, rain and fog blocked our course south, so I changed our flight plan and flew back to Lynn Lake, trying to go round the back of the weather front. No luck. I tried again, that same afternoon, this time flying over two hours before we ended back at Churchill. Tomorrow would be OK, said the weather man. "All blue skies. No problem." But next morning the snow came down thickly. Two days later we flew away from foggy Churchill. (Christ! I looked back and couldn't see the airport.) I detoured to the west of Lake Winnipeg, because there are more airfields that side. We kept on flying south via The Pas, Dauphin and Grand Forks, our overnight stop. Two hours on from Grand Forks the oil was coming back so thick I had to put down at St. Cloud and abandon the flight. They did a dye test, and found the crankshaft was cracked. "A sudden stop. Your airplane was nosed over at some time," they opined. "Your prop would have come off in another hour." We drove home in a rented car. It had been a fun trip, some of the time.

Lessons of trip

Don't trust weather forecasts.
Don't trust engine log books.
Don't fly passengers over uninhabited areas.

10-3. A JUNKET TO MEXICO

<u>Winter</u>

January, 1969. N3372D was parked on the apron at Aurora, Illinois, in below-zero weather. For a long hour the clear ice was laboriously scraped from the wings while the engine was preheated for starting. Airborne, the airplane circled stiff-jointed over the frozen ponds while I air-tested her prior to flying south to Mexico. I calibrated the new magnetic compass and tracked the Davenport beacon on the ADF. Next week the plane was booked for its fourth trip to the radio shop for work on the aging radios – but when the time came it was too cold for our car to start to get to the airfield. Another week dragged by. Now the airplane's engine wouldn't start – they had run the battery right down in installing a new starter drive; ice was floating in the cells. I bumped into an airport acquaintance. "We've sold everything and are moving to Arizona," he told me. The Cessna 180 sat in the cold waiting the day of departure, February 15, 1969.

<u>To Kitty Hawk</u>

More snow was predicted for Chicago Saturday morning, so on Friday night I went to the airfield, marked a course to Dayton, and left. (I was flying solo. I'd arranged to pick up Helen in Florida, where she was visiting her parents.) There was no moon. I couldn't find Montgomery Field – or couldn't get the lights to come on – where Helen's relatives would put me up, so I landed at Middletown, twenty miles away. Next day, under cold, gloomy skies (my mood to match), I flew over West Virginia's death-mask landscape to Kitty Hawk. Landing at First Flight Airport, I walked in the cold wind to the site of the 1903 flight. A belt of snow and freezing rain barred my flight south and caused me to wait out two days at Elizabeth City.

<u>To Key West</u>

Tuesday morning I was at the grass field early. It was raining. I roared off the field, and flew low over Albemarle Sound, heading south. It was misty going, but the sun came out at the Florida state line as I circled Okefenoke Swamp. At Clearwater Beach I picked up Helen, and we flew over the orange groves to Homestead, and then by way of the Everglades to Key West, arriving 4.00P.

Over the Gulf

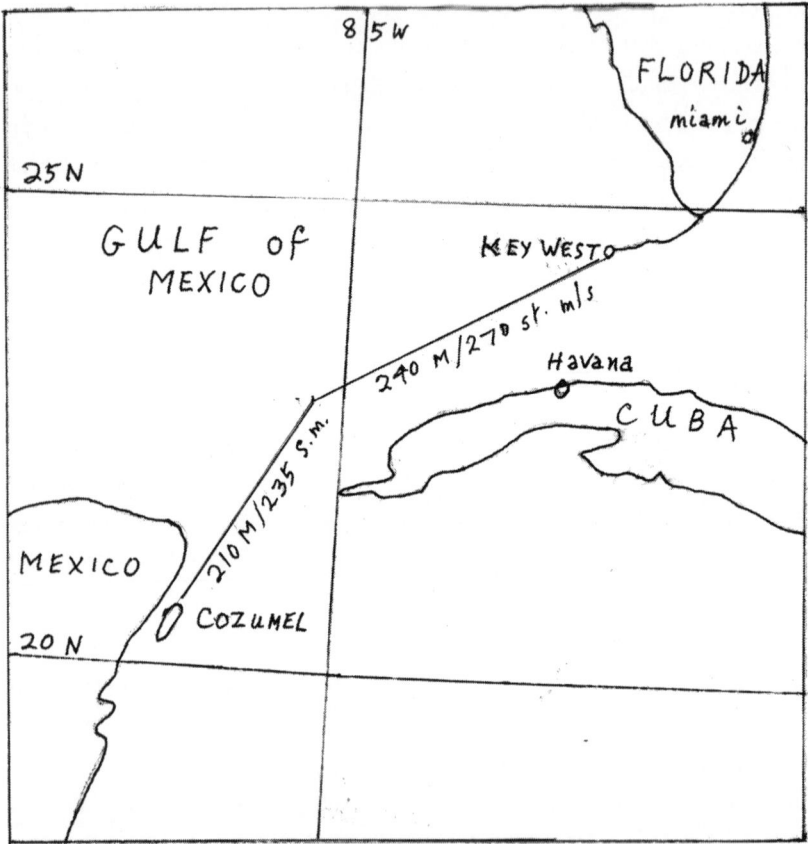

The over-water distance from Key West to the island of Cozumel is 450 miles. The satellite photo showed the route to be cloudy, but free of major weather systems. We rose two hours before dawn, got the winds (they were northerly), calculated a dead reckoning course, and headed out across the Gulf into nothingness. (Not to worry. I had a newly majored engine.) The

180 was steady enough at 6,000 feet to fly hands off. Ignoring the fickle ADF, I steered 240 on the magnetic compass. After two hours, presumably having passed clear of Cuba – we were above broken clouds – I turned to 210 M, which included ten degrees allowance so as to prejudice our landfall to the Yucatan Peninsula, rather than pass it by to the east. The dead reckoning was correct, though the sight of a coast line (through a hole in the clouds) was unanticipated. I had neglected to figure that our adjusted heading would bring us to land some twenty minutes earlier than had our landfall been Cozumel. "It's too early for land," I said. Only three hours had elapsed since take off. "Cuba," guessed Helen, who had been listening to Havana on the VHF. We skimmed down to 500 feet, and looked around. "Let's head south and see if this is an island." It wasn't. It was the mainland, not Cuba. Soon we picked up CZM beacon, and crossed over to Cozumel.

"You come to Mejico in that leetle thing? You must be very brave!" (tr. "Only a fool would do that.")

After 24 hours on the opulent island of Cozumel (three Lockheed Jetstars at the airfield; a full-rigged ship in the harbor), we flew to Chichen-Itza, to see the Mayan ruins. Landing at the unattended airfield there, our tail wheel snapped off. What to do now? We waited until an itinerant airplane landed, and Helen approached the pilot and asked him, in Spanish, for help. He very kindly had the part sent down from Mexico City and a mechanic from Merida, both of which arrived next day. Meanwhile we looked at the ruins and at the encroaching rain forest, with its orchids, humming birds, tarantulas, and painted buntings.

Two days to Mexico City

After an overnight stay at Villahermosa, parked near twelve Cessna 180 air taxis, we left, only to turn back short of Minatitlan because of fog and land back at Villahermosa. It wasn't good south either, said a 180 taxi pilot. But we went high over the clouds to Tuzla Gutierrez on the strength of the actual reports, and then, as the clouds started breaking up, west to Ixtepec and on to a landing at Oaxaca. Flying airplanes is great! From Oaxaca, a relatively high flight, at 12,500 feet, to Mexico City. Breathing from an oxygen bottle, we homed on Popocatepetel, visible 125 miles away. From Mexico City, we took a side trip – taking Helen's mother along – to Guanajuato (elev. 6,500 feet) to see the colonial town.

To Tucson

Leaving Helen in Mexico with her parents, I headed north. From Mazatlan, I beach-combed along the Gulf of California, flying lower than the frigate birds, over the fishermen in their colored boats. That palling, I turned inland at Los Mochis, and headed 250 miles on the diagonal across the Sierra Madre mountains, more or less along the route of the spectacular Copper Canyon railroad. At Chihuahua, after a jolting ride, I visited Pancho Villa's house, paying a small entrance fee to his widow (yes, there had been a big age difference!). From there, I refueled at Nuevo Casas Grandes, passing the Sierra del Nido, reputedly the last home in Mexico (1962) of the grizzly bear. There was snow on the relatively low (9,000 feet) peak overlooking a ranch marked as Hacienda Casa de Adobe; I was approaching winter again. I paid 200 pesos "extra" to get an exit visa, because the customs officer's idea of the forms required in Nogales differed from those of the officials in Cozumel.

Back to Winter

After stopping to tour the Saguaro National Monument, I was ready to leave Tucson. The weather map showed "ridges of high pressure," and the outlook purported to show that I could take a more or less direct route to Chicago. In accordance with this outlook, I rashly crossed over the high country of the Colorado Plateau. Near Four Corners, I encountered 80 mph winds and snow showers that sent me scurrying for an airport. I wasn't too sure where I was, but thought I could get into Durango. Things were getting worse when I made it into Farmington, NM. Snow had reached the airfield boundary as I made my approach to land. After two days there I was able to leave for La Junta via the scenic San Luis Valley. Blanca Peak had a lenticular cloud in its lee. From La Junta, I flew 500 miles non-stop over blinding white ground snow to Kansas City. An ice storm was forecast so I parked my Cessna and took a jetliner to Chicago.

As to my flight through Mexico…God! I enjoyed that trip!

Ch. 10. America as playground? I was forced to fly lower and lower, as snow and 80 mph winds near Four Corners sent the 180 scurrying for Farmington, NM, March 1969. The Colorado plateau is salmon pink, the color of Navajo sandstone (image reversed).

Ch.11. PT-19. Better than riding a roller coaster. Pilot Aurora (front seat) and Helen (rear seat) stunting over Brazil, 1969. Note rollover pylon between cockpits.

11

"FLYING DOWN TO RIO"

I have to say that my trip to Rio was more humdrum than the preposterous musical film of that name, starring Fred Astaire and Ginger Rogers (there were no wing-walking dancing girls), but I have vivid memories of the sessions stunting in a PT-19 over the *campos* of Rio Grande do Sul. What's more, I still have the aerial shots on 8mm movie film I made from a Super Cub of a PT-19 somersaulting the tilting horizon, against the vast backdrop of blue sky, red earth, and green field crops. It's not that I haven't flown aerobatics before or since. It's that words are not always the best medium for depicting flight, and that the movie film brings back the exhilaration of that particular locale and time.

At the end of 1970 I had gone to Brazil and spent four months on a consulting assignment for the UN, splitting my time between several places but spending much time in Rio de Janeiro and Rio Grande do Sul. Brazil is a sort of Portuguese version of the United States, except it had then a military government. It was the place for barbecue ("*churrasco*"), and the everpresent ten thousand cruzeiro note, worth about two U.S. dollars, a colorful piece of paper money that depicted Santos-Dumont in his 14-*bis* airplane, and over-stamped "10", which represented the cumulative devaluation of the currency to the time of issue.

For this assignment I had to fly in commercial airplanes to get around that big country. Also, I interrupted my main business to make an interim flight from

Rio to Bogota, Colombia, which entailed flying, twice, over 1,600 miles of rain forest with an intermediate landing at Manaus beside the Amazon. And I visited Campo Grande in the state of Matto Grosso, where I saw the hump-backed cattle in the fields, & the tall, coffee-colored girls walking in town.

My favorite work location was at Sao Leopoldo, in Rio Grande do Sul, where there was an aero club that had, among other airplanes, a couple of Fairchild PT-19s (WW2-vintage low wing, open cockpit monoplanes, with plywood wings). I had hoped to rent one of these planes, and I visited the air ministry in Rio to get a flying permit on the basis of my FAA license – and was practically thrown out by the colonel in charge of that department. (No permit for you!) It would have been easy, I was told at the flying club, if I had used an intermediary, a *despachante* (a fixer), who works for a fee. "In *Brasil*, never ask for anything directly!"

Although I wasn't permitted to solo the club's planes, I flew in half-a-dozen types of aircraft and got over five hours dual in the Fairchild, and it was marvelous. One of the pilots was named Aurora, the other, Cavedon. "Air show aerobatics" I noted in my log book: loops, chandelles, spins, lazy eights, slow rolls, Immelmans.

Ch. 12. Tailwind N64855 at snowy Clow Field. Illinois, March 1975. The Tailwind, a 1953 design, is one of the most successful experimental aircraft. I figured I'd get 160 mph if I installed a seventy-inch pitch propeller. But Steve Wittman, the designer, scotched that idea: "You'll never get off the ground," he told me. Why the Sioux Indian on the fuselage? High spirits, that's all.

12

HOMEBUILT AIRPLANES
1971-1975

Happiness is building your own airplane

When I returned from Brazil in January 1971, I was too short of funds to buy a reliable used airplane, even one of those 1946 models with mice in the wings. ("I can hear them squeaking," said owner Al Campbell, "so it must be time to rebuild.") It was then that I listened to the blandishments of the designers of "homebuilts," exciting little air planes (plans only $50) that could be built, it was claimed, in a year's worth of weekends and for more or less pocket money. A vision triumphant appeared to me: pistons sliding, propeller whirring, controls deflecting... I decided to build an airplane. As it turned out, a good part of the next four years went into building two of them, and I spent thousands of hours confined to my garage and to drafty barns and hangars in the process. (I was also working intermittently at a consulting firm in nearby Oak Brook.)

Even then, before the advent of "kit planes," there was a wide choice of designs, ranging from marginal types to super-planes, representing an exorbitant input of time, skill, and money. One of the corps of would-be airplane constructors (the man with mice in his airplane's wings) had set his heart on building "a plane that will look like a Demoiselle going backwards." When one considers that Santos-Dumont's famous plane was a weak flyer at best, he could only wonder at the erratic progress of ideas. As for me, I would be happy with a thoroughly conventional airplane – just like the one I had seen at nearby Clow Field, near Naperville. It was an open-cockpit monoplane, like the Bleriot XI, or like a scaled-down Fairchild. This was Fly Baby, a design by Boeing engineer Peter Bowers from Seattle. It had a 65-HP engine, a wing span of twenty-eight feet, and was built from Sitka Spruce. Fly Baby, which won the 1962 EAA Design Contest, owed something to Bleriot and much to the 1930s and 1940s. (It would come to pass that I would build the Fly Baby, paint her Cub-yellow, and fly her, one memorable Sunday morning, over the Sears Tower in downtown Chicago. Dreams do come true.)

I contacted the builder of the plane I had seen at Clow Field, Bill Cahill, who lived in nearby La Grange. Yes, he would help me, said Bill, and so I became apprentice to just the right man, an enthusiastic craftsman who could talk knowledgeably about boss and gear transmissions, roll-forming equipment, and technologies ranging far from the simple Fly Baby. This was a new and stimulating world, full of practical, up-beat people preoccupied with making things. Get two or three of these Chicagoans around a table, and they would outdo one another in figuring out the manufacturing process for everything in sight: the ashtray, the coffee spoon, the door knob, the table and the chairs. "Give me a vertical milling machine any day," Bill would enthuse. "To heck with the horizontal."

I got the plans in the mail from the designer in Seattle, and I started my project on the first day of July 1971 by driving to Chicago's 95th Street, to B & F Aircraft Supply. This Midwest institution, a cluttered shop topped by a tattered windsock, was owned by two old-timers, Foose and Cartwright, "the both of them" made in the mold of Scrooge and Marley. It had been a repair shop that was left high and dry when the adjoining air strip was built over, some years before. Part of the shop's inventory (wire wheels from a Curtiss Jenny, and so forth) dated from the time "when Charles Lindbergh was popping jelly beans between flights at Checkerboard airmail field in nearby Maywood." Here at B & F I was met with the scorn appropriate to the novice, a state quickly revealed by my uninformed attempt to purchase a bill of materials for the Fly Baby. "We don't sell *longerons*; we sell *planks* of standard dimension. *You* do the figuring and the cutting."

For my main spruce supply, I drove to the Wicks Organ Factory in East St Louis, Illinois. They had railway car loads of the finest selected spruce (raw material for their sounding boards) in a siding adjacent to the factory. The manager – a Fly Baby builder himself – helped me pick out main and rear wing spars. Building a wooden airplane, it was suggested, had many similarities to building a piano: the tools (wood saw, rasps, dozens of clamps); the supplies (wood, varnish, glue); and the methods (layout jigs, lamination of wood strips). The bible for this process – the fruit of years of trial and error – was the old Civil Aeronautics Manual CAM 18, which included in its mass of detail the maximum permitted deviation of the wood grain inclination in a spar and much else besides, including the standards for cutting 4130 steel with a hacksaw. (Steel has a grain, too.)

I was now started on a new and all-consuming activity, vaguely aware that the labors in my garage were multiplied ten thousand times throughout the country by other hammer-wielding gnomes, yearning for the freedom of the air. (What luck that I had time and the opportunity and, above all, the technical advice from Bill Cahill, to build that airplane!) Eventually, my evolving project spilled out of my garage into the old milk barn on Boyd Clow's farm-cum-airfield. There I came to know others in the special collection of people who make up experimental aviation, or at least those in Chapter 86 of EAA: super-hobbyists, airplane addicts, pundits, kibitzers, volunteer helpers, hangers-on, tinkerers, perfectionists, perennial adolescents, as well as a large, out-of-focus group whom Cahill surmised had been on their way to a meeting of the Isaak Walton League, and had unaccountably stopped over at the airport. Out of this multitude of enthusiasts, there was a hard core who were committed to building airplanes. "I can get you fifty pilots for every one of those," said Bill, exaggerating.

I tell you, we didn't look like much. (Not like Clark Gable, anyway. "He was a sight to see in his perfectly fitting uniform," I've been told. "A fine looking man, and a swell guy to know, to boot. He had sixteen Parker shotguns." Gable, an air gunner on a B-17, was Hitler's favorite movie star, such that Hitler offered a reward for his capture.) As I got to know them, I realized that they were all high rollers, these airplane nuts. In pursuit of their dream of flight, some would lose their wives, their jobs, and even their lives. Old, young, fat, thin, poor, rich (correction: there were no rich among us), the dream was the thing.

I wondered how we compared with the backyard builders of sixty years before? Several blacksmiths made early and unsuccessful airplanes here in Illinois. Like them, perhaps, several of our group were longer on mechanical aptitude than science. Joe Schweitzer would certainly have been building some of those wildly original airplanes had he been active at an earlier time. So went my line of thinking one oppressively hot evening as Joe and I sat in his garage drinking whisky and water from quart-sized pickle jars (that would have been even better suited to raising tadpoles). A foreman in the locomotive works, Joe had completed one airplane and was well along with his second. Both planes, it was alleged, had an uncommonly large number of steam fittings (!) and confounded his peers by the complexity of their systems. One of the nicest, most unassuming people on Clow Field, Joe had the tough appearance of a bar-room denizen over whose noggin dozens of bottles could be broken without effect. Listening to his surprising interpretations of aerodynamics, one could believe that dozens of merely conventional principles had been broken over his head with equal lack of results.

As I recall, Joe's second, as yet uncompleted, airplane was more unorthodox than the first, but even that one flew in a queer rudder-twitchy way, presumably because Joe had deviated from the plans by doubling the area of the rudder. (It was a type of homebuilt with all the vices of a Sopwith Camel and none of its performance.) The second airplane I had come to see had the beginnings of a retractable gear system, which Joe had been testing when I arrived at his house that evening. Like the old woman that lived in a shoe – and like a surprising number of pilots – Joe had so many children he didn't know what to do with them most of the time. This day, though, he employed them to good effect; they pushed him down the street, in his uncompleted airplane, which rested on a dolly, while Joe raised and lowered the gear. More gulps of whisky…I remained baffled by the new plane. A parody ran through my head: "The flying machine, which has been looked upon for centuries as a thing to be laughed at, is now recognized as a coming method of transportation, the change in public sentiment dating from the day when the news came that Mr. Jos. Schweitzer, an Illinois manufacturer of locomotives, flew from one side of Lake Michigan to the other in a machine of his own design."

And there was John Friling. He finished three airplanes during the time that I knew him at Clow Field. His method of constructing his original-design aircraft was identical to that of the early builders such as Fokker; John built by eye, without plans, and – I was startled to find – couldn't tell me the wing span measurement of the latest plane that he had built. This design, a tandem-seat, parasol monoplane, would not fly at first; the center of gravity was too far back, and the airplane couldn't get its tail up for take-off. John took a welding torch and moved the engine and landing gear ten inches forward, and the plane flew well. He called this plane *Sumthin'r'other*.

Such freedom from supervision evidently makes Europeans nervous. One of my German colleagues at Mega Bank – this was a couple of years later – wouldn't believe that flying could be conducted in such a free and easy fashion as at Clow Field. (Does his government sign off every morning that he's got his pants on straight?)

"Well, did you play with Rudy today?" Helen would ask, artlessly, on my return from the airfield. Rudy Ficek was our King of Toys. When I knew him, he had three airplanes, two motor boats, a couple of canoes, a camper-trailer, a jeep, and twenty-six sporting rifles. A sort of local Friar Tuck, Rudy not only looked the part (though he was quite short, he weighed in at 307 lbs.) but actually combined a religious bent (he had been a missionary in Brazil) with a passion for diversion. It should be mentioned that much of his mystique derived from his situation as a union machinist on indefinite paid leave from GM; freedom judiciously exercised – he was reputed to know every blueberry patch for a hundred miles around.

No dream of flight was stronger than Earl Magnus's particular dream of finishing and flying his Fly Baby. He set himself a fast pace in his workshop, shaping wood and tightening bolts to the rousing music of John Philip Sousa, marching to the music while the glue dried and the doped fabric tightened. He was motivated, he confided, by his fear of dying prematurely, like his father. (I shared his conviction that we were all short of time.) Like Rudy, Earl Magnus was a noted trencherman (he and Rudy were the terror of the "all you can eat" smorgasbord restaurants) and a super-hobbyist. I recall hearing his mother complain of her fifty-four-year old son, "One time it was ham radio – aerials everywhere; then scuba diving – nothing mattered unless it was underwater; now airplanes – everything's got to be up in the air!" "You forgot the boats," I reminded her. "Also, the black-powder pistols."

Like me, Earl was building a Fly Baby, and it was said that he was building the nicest, cheapest, and most expensive airplane around. Cheap because Earl was a champion scrounger of materials. You couldn't drive down a suburban street with Earl without stopping somewhere to pre-empt the junk man in retrieving from the curb some such item as a washing machine: "Good for spare parts," he'd say. Earl sold me a metal propeller for fifteen dollars that he bought at auction after it was left at a railway station. (I bolted it to the engine of my Fly Baby – you can see it on the cover of this book.) On the other hand, Earl's plane was expensive because he spent so much time on his airplane project that his commission income (he sold light fixtures so as to keep his schedule as open as possible) was at an all-time low. But did anyone get more out of life than Earl? Not that I've seen.

Earl's saving grace – and that of his friends – was this: we knew we were oddballs and, unlike Octave Chanute when he introduced Wilbur Wright to the Western Society of Engineers, didn't trouble to deny it. (It was here in Chicago on September 18, 1901, in the Monadnock Building on Adams Street, that Mr. Wilbur Wright read his paper, "Some Aerial Experiments.") Odd or not, we were proving some kind of point. "Anyone," said Bill Cahill, "who says people can't do things with their hands anymore, just doesn't know what he's talking about. Here is a plumber," he continued, standing beside a particularly fine homebuilt airplane, "who has built a flying machine to a standard requiring the dexterity of a surgeon. Yet most people cannot conceive of a talented plumber."

I was unusual among the airplane builders at Clow Field – many of whom were tradesmen, mechanics, or engineers – in that I had little or no background in mechanics. Bill liked to tell how, in our early association, I approached him brandishing a screwdriver, "Oy sy, Bill, 'ow do I use this 'ammer?" Well, Bill had always been around tools – he was currently working as a high-school shop instructor. And he had the knack of completing a job with whatever tools were at hand. He would be helping someone with a project, and the right tool wouldn't be there. "I've got just the tool at home," an onlooker would volunteer. "And I understand," Bill would retort, "that they've got a lot of tools in Australia. But they won't help us here!"

However manifested, the effort that went into these homebuilt airplanes was extraordinary. "Seven years, eight months and three days," a graying Fly Baby builder (he happened to be a retired prison guard, and particularly sensitive, one supposed, to the passage of time) told me it took him to get to the first flight. Ten years was not uncommon. A simple airplane could take thousands of hours to build. (This was before the days of pre-manufactured "kit planes" that are assembled rather than built.) In the real world, the non-hobbyist's world, people don't have that kind of free time. Unlike us, their diversions are on the margin of the page, not in the center.

As I was building my airplane, I was reassured by its robust design: the fact that Fly Baby's main truss consisted of main spars of spruce 3/4 inch wide by 5 1/2 inch deep braced by eight flying wires and eight landing wires, each of 1/8 inch X 19 strand, one-ton stainless steel cable, anchored to 3/16 inch 4130 steel fittings and tensioned by turnbuckles of appropriate specifications (see Civil Aeronautics Manual 18, 1943). Concerning "landing wires": their function is to brace the wings of a monoplane, as illustrated in the photos of Fly Baby in this book. Very early on, Bleriot discovered that the death of five pilots had been caused by wing collapse as a result of negative G imposed when the pilots pushed the control stick forward. Evidently the cables used as landing wires were not up to the job.

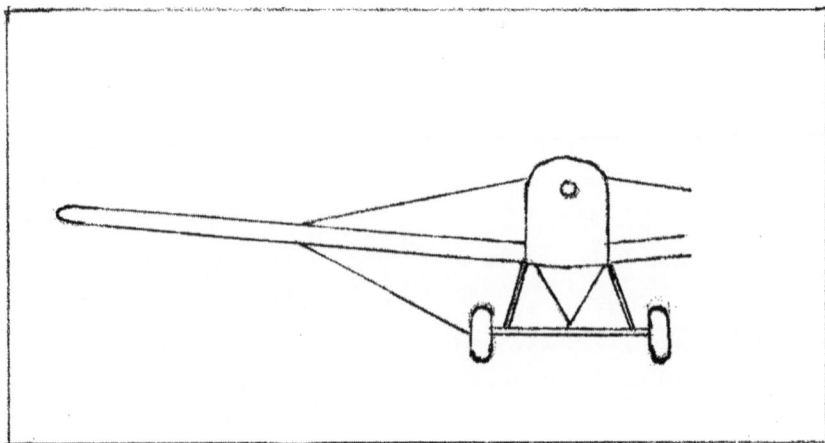

Bowers Fly Baby
Wire-braced wings & tail, 4 flying & 4 landing wires (1 ton ea.) support
main spar; same for rear spar. Rigid landing gear, 8.00 X 4 tires.

Still, airplanes crashed. *Home-Made Plane Falls; Flyer Dies* reported the
Chicago *Tribune*, of the death of 21-year old Michael Seymour of the
adjoining Naperville Aero Estates. He was killed moments after takeoff, on
the airplane's maiden flight. "It was constructed with excellent workman-
ship," reported his friends. "It is really a shame," the news item concluded.
"If he'd had 20 feet more altitude he might have made it."

After a year's work, almost 2,000 hours, my Fly Baby was structurally complete, standing on its landing gear, the wings on and the controls hooked
up: a beautiful skeleton (to my eye) of varnished wood and chromated steel.
Bowers records his total labor time to flying status as 720 hours. Better mul-
tiply that by three or four times. (It depends on your experience, how you
record your time, and how many spare parts you have.) I kept time sheets
for both my airplanes. I figured I had done eighty to ninety percent of the
work on Fly Baby, but that didn't include Bill's time and skill in welding
the landing gear and the elevator controls, and his help in twenty other
ways. Without Bill there would have been no project. (When I'd finished the

plane – I have to relate this against myself – Bill said casually, "Do you have any use for that belt sander, now you're done?" "I think I'd better hold on to it," I replied. That was the deal, then: I returned his generosity by quibbling over a lousy belt sander.)

Meanwhile, I had driven with Cliff Pond all the way to the suburbs of Washington D.C. to bring back a 75 HP Continental engine for my Fly Baby; and typical of experimental-grade engines, it wasn't all it was made out to be. With help from Earl and volunteers from EAA Chapter 86, which was based at Clow Field, I succeeded in getting the 1939-vintage Continental engine to run for the first time after its overhaul (an overhaul that was a saga in itself). After interminable prop swinging, there was a stuttering burst of power, piston slap, then muffled shouts of "Shut down! No oil pressure!" and finally the sweet sound of a sustained burst of power. It only remained to clothe the skeleton of the airplane in Dacron fabric (from an envelope sewn by Helen) and to secure this cloth to the wing ribs using a twelve-inch needle and nylon thread; to dope and paint the fabric; to fashion the cowling from aluminum sheet; and to complete the weight and balance calculations on this oversized model airplane. (Empty weight would be 697 lbs.) This took another six months, and I had the airplane inspected by the FAA inspector on 19 January 1973. He noted 13 "discrepancies," including the need to safety specific bolts and to placard particular valves and gauges. After I did this, my airplane received a Special Airworthiness Certificate on 31 January, 1973.

Now I wrenched my attention from building to flying. First, there was the mandatory medical, pivotal to which was a rectal examination – an inglorious procedure, aggravated by its apparent lack of connection with flight above the clouds. Then, when I arranged to practice circuits and landings in an old Taylorcraft, I broke off the tail wheel in a clumsy landing. Next I acquired the gear for open-cockpit, winter flying: a goose-down-insulated suit, fleece-lined ski boots, heavy gloves, goggles, a ski-mask and a motorcycle helmet with visor. (Expected wind chill effect was 10F.) The recommended method for test flying a single-seat airplane is to taxi fast along the runway a few times without leaving the ground; then, on subsequent runs to coax her into the air for short hops; and finally to commit the airplane to full flight. (A sound procedure: years later I watched the entire tail unit break away from a fiberglass airplane during the course of such high-speed runs – and no-one was hurt.) This procedure I followed, and found myself, February 2, 1973, cruising over the wintry landscape (the snow lying thick in the woods and on north-facing slopes). My airplane was a big yellow hawk, looking down on the hunters and their dogs walking across the fields. It was an anti-climax to descend, climb out of the plane, and share the view of a field mouse which can't see over the tops of things.

My new plane, N2685, had flown well, though with one wing low, and this condition I corrected by adjusting the tension of the turnbuckles on the wing bracing wires such that the angle of incidence was increased on the low wing. I spent much of March and April 1973, cavorting in the strong winds – sometimes harmlessly scraping the sturdy wing tips on the tarmac runway. This type of airplane really can be flown "by the seat of the pants." Bill Cahill told me he could initiate a slow, skidding turn in the Fly Baby by stretching out one hand, palm facing front, into the slipstream. It was an easy plane to fly. A friend, an airline pilot, barrel rolled my plane over the airfield the very first time he took her up.

I liked to loop, because it is an easy maneuver, and I enjoyed pitching forward in a wire-singing dive, pulling the airplane on to her back while I tilted my head back to see the opposite horizon come into view. Later that spring, when Bill Cahill took his Fly Baby out of winter storage, we got into mischief by steeple chasing over the countryside together, wind roaring in our faces, and buzzing sports cars, at a safe distance, on country roads. On one of these days, following Bill into a farmer's field, I struck a power line with my landing gear. The Fly Baby slowed like a shot bird and, lucky for me, flopped into the field right side up. Both wooden vees of the landing gear were scored, and five farms lost their power. "I could see that you were going to hit those wires," said the farmer, after we'd landed, "and there was nothing I could do about it."

I should have guessed that Bill Cahill, a gregarious man, played the piano. This came to light when Bill came to supper at the home of friends of mine, a respectable couple in Glen Ellyn. Spying an upright piano in the next room, Bill asked if he might play. The hostess, expecting a few bars of Cole Porter, assented, and was thrown off balance when Bill launched into a loud boogie beat. This encouraged another guest, Bill Chambers, a veteran of flying the Hump no less, to sit down on the same bench and pound the same keyboard. The two Bills were making a heck of a row. Our hostess, Mrs. Clifford Pond, was clearly flustered playing the part of Margaret Dumont opposite the Marx Brothers in "A Night at the Opera." We could see that we'd overstayed our time, so we said thanks and goodbye and left in our respective automobiles.

During 1973 I flew the Fly Baby on two over-night trips from Lombard to Troy, MI, to visit my in-laws. Both round-trip flights took 7 ½ hours with a ground speed of 70 mph. I loved open-cockpit flying!

After only one hundred wonderful hours of flying my brand-new airplane, I sold her, for the cost of materials, to a man from Davenport, IA, who approached me at Clow Field one day with an offer to buy the Fly Baby. (I flew it down for him.)

Why on earth did I sell my plane? One: I wanted a faster, two-place airplane; Two: I was now addicted to airplane construction; Three: I had my eye on a "ninety percent completed" project, a Wittman Tailwind, owned by an airline pilot down the road, who had a second Tailwind. Four: I needed the cash to buy an engine, an 0-200 supposedly "like new" for the Tailwind. What can I say? I wouldn't do it again. At the time, though, I had no remorse, and plunged back into the workshop spending time and money I couldn't afford – all without consulting Helen. Bill, I think, saw the situation as it was, but all he said, over a beer at the American Legion, was something on the theme *per ardua ad astra*. He was flirting with "aspiration", the very essence of flight. He was groping for the intangible. He philosophized: "When you've made the first flight, the thrill is ninety percent over." (That ninety percent figure again.)

So, back to our garage in Wheaton, then back to the hangar at Clow Field, and I worked fairly continuously on the Tailwind from July 1973 to February 1975 (perhaps a thousand hours). I covered the fuselage and wings in "Razorback" fiberglass in a shed with a portable heater. Foose checked the welds on the control linkages. I was likely to be in the unheated hangar doing the mechanical work any day when the temperature exceeded 20F. It was a cold, dark hangar, and I worked with an extension light. A typical job – taking several hours – was hooking up the brakes. Hydraulic fluid would spill on the floor, and my chilled hands were cut by cotter pins. But it was all I wanted to do. (I was, after all, an addict.) And there were challenging problems to solve. What sort of propeller should I use on the 0-200 Continental? I calculated that with a pitch of seventy inches, I could attain a top speed of 160 mph, and I telephoned Wittman, the designer, in Wisconsin, to confirm this. Wittman, whose flying license was signed by Orville Wright, told me, "With a pitch of seventy inches, you'll never get off the ground." [Steve Wittman was killed flying a Tailwind variant some years later, in 1995, at the age of ninety-one.]

I test flew the Tailwind at Clow Field, and before the year was out, flew it to Washington D.C., to take up a new job. The Tailwind, N64855, I painted in the colors of the Lafayette Escadrille, with a screaming Sioux Indian in war bonnet on the fuselage. (The personnel department of the Bank hadn't specified arrival in an experimental airplane as an impediment to hiring. Nor in my fast passage low across Ohio, would a rustic rifleman see me fly over, fire by reflex, and put a bullet through my airplane, as had happened to Steve Wittman's Tailwind.)

Even before I test flew the Tailwind, Al Neunteufel of Chapter 101 crashed his new Thorp monoplane near Addison, Illinois. (He was enough of a pal of mine that I had let him take up my Fly Baby.) The crash was a double tragedy, as Al's neighbor's daughter was along for the fatal flight. That was in August 1974. Meanwhile, things were beginning to unravel a bit at Clow Field. Chapter 86's Fly Baby, a communal project, was wrecked by a novice pilot after only four hours total flying time. Then, Bill Cahill's Fly Baby was broken in half when hit by a spam can (a Cessna, I think), which taxied on to the runway threshold and into Bill's landing path. "It was a shock," Bill confessed, "like when I came home last week and found a bill of divorcement on the kitchen table."

Next was Earl's turn. "I was approaching to land at Lockport in very gusty conditions when my Fly Baby encountered wind shear, and flipped upside down. I was looking straight down at the ground, so I pushed the stick against the side of the cockpit by reflex, rolled upright, and landed straight ahead. 'That was great trick flying you did!' someone said, thinking that it was a deliberate maneuver. That evening," Earl continued, "I happened to accompany my wife to a séance. The reader told her that in her former life, Mad [Madeleine, Earl's wife] had lived in ancient Egypt. 'What about me?' I asked. 'You were a World War One pilot,' the reader told me. 'So what happened?' 'You got killed,' she said."

"Now you tell me," said Earl, "how she knew I am a pilot? The very next time I went up, I groundlooped the Fly Baby. The landing gear sheared off, and the airplane slid along on its belly until she hit a ditch and flipped over on her back. So far, so bad. I was suspended upside down in my harness, a foot above the ground. Well, I was sure I could hold myself in the seat by jamming my knees against the side of the cockpit. But when I pulled the quick release, I slid out on my head. Ouch! I got the message. It was time to sell this plane and fly *model* airplanes." [That's what Earl did.]

I flew the Tailwind for a hundred hours, testing her under various sandbag loadings, different stabilizer angles, and at various flap settings. I bought and tested two custom-made wooden props (62 D 65 P and 64 D 63 P). It was absorbing work. On September 27, 1975, I made a 625-mile cross-country flight to Eagle River, WI, averaging 140 mph, "dirty", without wheel pants or fairings. This was less than I had hoped, but speedy enough, twice the speed of the Fly Baby. (The forests that day were a blaze of fall color.) After I moved to Virginia, I parked the airplane at Leesburg Field. Soon enough that shiny 0-200 engine I had bought from the airline pilot broke down. I stored the Tailwind in my barn until I sold the little airplane a few years later to a man from Baltimore.

Note: I built Fly Baby N2685 from scratch for a total of $3,250 including the overhauled 75HP Continental engine. (Those were the days!) First flight was Feb. 3, 1973 after I had spent 2,650 hours in construction. Overall, for my two homebuilt airplanes, I spent twenty "building" hours to one "flying" hour. Then, with regret, I quit building airplanes and took the first available job, which happened to be in Washington, DC.

Ch. 12. Amateur flyers have most of the fun in the air, I noticed. Earl Magnus of EAA, Sh. 86, in his Bowers Fly Baby, 1974, with Rudy Ficek swinging the prop. Along with the capacity for merriment was the powerful aspiration to soar into the sky.

13

FLYING LIKE THE HAWKS
(AMERICA AS PLAYGROUND)

The favored wind of the best glider pilots, the hawks, is a nor'wester in the fall of the year. Then they can make a swift passage along the endless wooded slopes of the Appalachians, soaring in the lift on the windward side. When that wind is blowing it sweeps away the dirty air over Chicago (the visibility jumps from one and a half miles to fifty), and the front speeds toward the east at 500 miles per day. Many of our glider pilots were retrieved from Tennessee, as I recall. My own schedule didn't allow that sort of thing, and I was confined to looking for local thermals, but when I moved east to Virginia I was within driving distance of the ridge and valley country of Pennsylvania.

I got back into gliding at Warrenton, VA, in 1976. There I heard about Ridge Flights at State College, PA, and I drove there to check them out. This is storied country, very close to Bellefonte, formerly a stop on the Washington – Cleveland route in the early days of the airmail, when they were flying the D.H.4. The Washington terminus was College Park, MD, and the mission completion rate was fifty per cent – the Liberty engine didn't have all the bugs worked out. (See Dean Smith's exuberant memoir *By the Seat of My Pants*.)

It was a long drive from McLean, VA to State College, PA, especially on my schedule, but I made seven trips in July/August 1976 (taking my family along), and sixteen solo flights (a couple of which were in excess of two hours) flying the ridge. I even bought a half-share in a Schweitzer 1-26, a pretty little single-seat sailplane. When the wind was conducive to ridge soaring, the procedure, according to Tom Knauff, was to fly fairly slowly, at 45 mph, and not to get on the lee side of the ridge. Tom had been owner and operator of Ridge Flights since 1975, and he subsequently set several world records there.

[The next year we bought a sailboat at Annapolis, which was a lot more practicable for me and the family. But I missed the gliding.]

14

THE BIG SQUEEZE

Davis Field was only minutes down Bethlehem Road from our house in the Manassas National Battlefield Park. I expected to fly frequently. But at the end of the year my tally of sporting sessions was: 83 riding, 13 trap and skeet, 11 sailing, 9 flying and 14 swimming. Add to that a lot of office work, and a couple of trips to sleepy old Egypt (forty-six days). I couldn't squeeze any more time out of the year, despite a temperament or personal history that compelled me to try.

The year (1982) started auspiciously in California, where we had spent Christmas with friends. We drove through Cajon Pass and came to an over-view of the Mojave Desert from where we could see the Sierra Nevada range and Mount Whitney, 150 miles away. Visibility was about 170 miles. I don't remember having seen farther. (In 1988 I flew a glider from there.)

Back in Washington, the first event of the New Year was the crash of Air Florida Flight 90, January 13, 1982. On that day it started snowing in the early afternoon, and I left work early to beat the traffic but decided to pull over and park at the Kennedy Center to stay clear of the snow plows. Shortly thereafter a Boeing 737 took off from National Airport with ice on its wings, failed to gain height, and hit the 14th Street Bridge. "Time 16.01. COPILOT: *This is it. We're going down, Larry.* CAPTAIN: *I know it.* [Sound of impact]." Seventy-eight persons were killed. It was overcast, snowing, dusk was settling in. All I could see and hear were flashing lights and the sound of sirens. It took a couple of hours before I-66 got plowed, and I could drive home.

I was happy to restrict myself to the slow-speed realm of sport flying.

1/24/1982. 1.1 hrs in Skyhawk with Robbie on a local photo shoot in bright sunshine. The whole countryside under deep, unmarked snow, like Newfoundland. No moving things to be seen. An immense glare filled the whole world.

2/12/1982. 2.2 hrs in Skyhawk, at night, with an instructor. Visibility unrestricted. From Manassas, we flew over the Washington metro area, landing at College Park, Gaithersburg, Warrenton, and Dulles airports. In this vast arena we swam through the night sky amid the navigation lights of other circling aircraft, enjoying the fireworks show of flashing lights from Washington National Airport, the Washington Monument and all the other lighted places. It's smooth flying at night. There's a sense of precariousness because the fields are black, and a forced landing – no problem in daylight – would not come off easily. But I love the lights. Paul Bewsher wrote a book in 1919, *The Adventures of a Night Bomber,* in which he reels off his impressions of "searchlights and star shells, flashes and glows, sunrises, moonglow, green and red Verey lights; and the white, moonlit beaches of the seacoast."

8/29/1982. 2.5 hours in Cessna 150 with Robbie. A peach of a day. Visibility was 100 miles plus. We flew to St. Mary's port on the Potomac River, cruised over Tangier Island, and saw bald eagles (but no airplanes) over the Yeocomico River.

I had motored our sailboat, *Kitty Hawk*, from Annapolis on Chesapeake Bay to Solomons Island for a season, and finally to convenient Neabsco Creek, on the Potomac River just off U.S. Route 1.

5/31/1982. Two hours sailing with Robbie. When beating against the wind in light airs, *Kitty Hawk* could only point about sixty degrees off the wind, instead of forty-five degrees. Our shallow draft boat draws only two feet, supposedly an advantage in shallower waters, but oh, for a centerboard! (I was clueless when I bought this boat.)

8/1/1982. Sailing three and a half hours with Robbie in good wind from the North.

9/5/1982. Now we know what *slow* is. With our outboard engine on the fritz, we spent nine and a half hours sailing from Nanjemoy Creek to Aquia Creek, *averaging one knot* with a light following wind, but against the tide.

More Thrills and Spills

For me, the only point of flying is for the thrill of it. Same with steeple chasing. Our neighbor Joan Jones, an equestrian version of Joan Hughes of White Waltham aerodrome, was Joint Master of the Bull Run Hunt of Manassas, Virginia. Under Joan's tutelage I spent four seasons, 1982-1986, hunting the meadows and woods east of Bull Run Mountain and further afield, chasing the red fox. Helen did a lot of riding, too, schooling her own horse and trail riding in the National Park. (We had four horses in all.) After considerable group schooling during an entire summer of long evenings, I ventured out early one morning with the young hounds. Almost immediately I was tossed off my horse, which galloped rider-less around the pasture as non-working horses grazed unperturbed nearby. This, and other humbling incidents – runouts, refusals, landing with a thump on top of a coop with forelegs on one side, hind legs on the other – Joan breezily pronounced, added up to "a very good day." Later I bought "Ralph," a horse of the two-speed variety: full out or full stop. But he was a "goer" and rarely refused a jump. (Up until then I tried out different horses, including "Spots", an Appaloosa, a breed of the Nez Perce Indians no less.) There were more than enough spills to keep me on my toes – an unruly version of flight training, and potentially as hazardous. Horses bolted; horses tossed me off. I practically pulled my arms out of their sockets. Horse trailers skidded off the icy roads. A lot of rough and tumble, more exciting than flying.

And there was steeple chasing, which explains a further gap in my desultory sport flying career. On the one hand, I thought, I might break my neck. On the other hand, Joannie assured me, "It only takes twenty minutes after you get started to go around the course, and you get to spend the rest of the day partying. Besides, we're not going for fast time." In 1983 and 1984, I teamed up with Joan to ride "pairs," with Joan in the lead, me following, on the point-to-point circuit. About a dozen other Hunts were represented. We competed over eight different courses in northern Virginia: Casanova, Rappahannock, Blue Ridge, Warrenton, Piedmont, Middleburg, Fairfax, and Old Dominion. A typical cross-country course was four miles and seventeen jumps. Casanova, the earliest of the races (held in February), had snow on the ground and poor footing at the jumps. The Blue Ridge meet was on a day of fierce north winds. (Charlie Fenwick, winner of England's Grand National, was riding that day.) At mountainous Rappahannock I rode Ralph close on the heels of Joannie's Warrior, whose hooves spattered my face with mud, while Joannie shouted instructions to me over her shoulder, "Downhill jump! Sit back!"

Of Piedmont, the *Chronicle of the Horse* reported that "the course is laid out over incredibly fine hunting country." In 1983, Joannie and I were No.6; Jackie Onassis and her partner, representing the Essex Fox Hounds, were No. 9, and so on, each pair's number pinned to our Melton coats.

The next year Joannie and I won first place overall for that season, optimum time. Thanks, Joannie!

Ch. 14 "Low flying": Riding "pairs" with Joannie Jones [R] at Middleburg races, 1983.

15

GLAMOUR... AND DISASTER

I flew three times on the Concorde in 1981 and 1982 (twice on BA and once on Air France). The Aerospatiale-BAC Concorde was a glamour queen that stayed in the spotlight for over thirty years until the type was grounded as the result of the fiery crash at Paris in the year 2000. She may have been, and some people think she was, the finest machine of any kind ever built. At any rate, Richard Collins, managing editor of *Flying* magazine, asserts that Concorde was the most remarkable airplane of all time. "This 400,000 lb airplane (of which 200,000 lb was fuel), routinely attained 58,000 ft altitude and Mach 2.1 in crossing the Atlantic." When you boarded the Concorde in London at noon to fly to Washington at twice the speed of sound, the ninety degree arc of longitude was traversed in 3hrs 45 mins, whereas the time difference between the two cities is five hours. (Best transatlantic speed for the Concorde was three hours.) After you'd flown in the Concorde, you weren't satisfied with any other aircraft. Too bad, because travel by SST is now a thing of the past.

The first jet airliner, the D.H. Comet, was a degree more glamorous than even the Concorde SST; and Comet first flew back in 1949, when I was at my most impressionable age. But pioneers get arrows in their backs, as the Americans say. There was the immense drama of the unexplained crashes of this advanced airplane. One can still see, in a small medieval church near my school on the North Downs, a wall tablet that commemorates the loss of a parishioner in the fall of the Comet off the Island of Elba in January

1954. The Comet fell in flames from 27,000 feet into the Tyrrhenian Sea. Catastrophic metal fatigue was the verdict of the coroner, who may or may not have been as familiar as we schoolboys with Milton's description of a like event: *Him the Almighty Power/ Hurled headlong flaming from the ethereal sky/ With hideous ruin and combustion, down/to bottomless perdition.*

This was the fourth "incident" with the Comet, and there was another crash to come. A big water tank was built belatedly at Farnborough in 1954 to test the Comet airframe to destruction. The Comet's commercial future was of course derailed, though after a re-design the type went on flying for fifty years. The Boeing 707 – and a very good airplane it was – cleaned up on the first phase of the jet airliner market. Pan Am was another beneficiary, until that glamorous airline stumbled during the 1973 oil crisis and was bank-rupted in 1991 as a result of mismanagement, high gas prices, over-regula-tion, and terrorism. At its zenith in the 1960s – when I took the helicopter from the top of the Pan Am building in Manhattan out to Kennedy, and on to Rome and Honolulu, back via San Francisco – the face of Pan Am was its corps of glamorous stewardesses: young, long-legged, curvaceous, dressed in blue. Who can forget them?

16

ESCAPE BY STRATAROCKET;
HELLO, GOD

At a time when the workaday BS (*Dict. of Slang* = *bold and deceitful absurdities*) was thick and deep, I was hailed by an acquaintance at a party. "Hullo, Flyboy! Want to buy a half-share in a Maule Stratarocket?" "Yes!" (The Maule is an STOL airplane manufactured in Moultrie, Georgia.)

This airplane, hangared at Midland airport on Route 28, added immeasurably to my outlook during the period 1984 to 1986. By flying a light airplane, I could disappear fast, if only for a short time across the Bay or the Blue Ridge. Owning a light airplane confers enormous mobility – and a state of mind: a gratifying sense of the potential of it, even when I was temporarily sitting at a desk.

Flying across the Bay took me an hour and fifteen minutes; driving, it could take five hours. The Maule was in the same class as the Cessna 180 tail dragger, with the same capability of landing in a small field, if that precaution were necessary. With the 220 HP Franklin engine, the Maule's rate of climb was rather better than the Cessna 180. I flew three times to Chicago in this airplane, and to Hot Springs, and Kitty Hawk and lots of places I'd like to go again, such as College Park, Crisfield, Bryce Canyon, and Falwell (I remember them all). Robbie was attending VES, a school in Lynchburg at the time. One end-of-term, I flew in to pick him up at Falwell. He showed up with two beefy friends and all their baggage, so I had to quickly refigure the weight and balance before we took off downhill from that little air strip.

It took 35 minutes to fly from Warrenton/Midland to College Park, around the DC beltway, cruising blithely over the automobiles competing grimly for their individual bits of roadway. It was pleasant to recall that College Park started operations in 1909 when it was a tramway ride from D.C., and that Wilbur Wright trained Signal Corps officers to fly from there. In 1918, the air mail service was inaugurated from College Park, flying war-surplus D.H. 4 airplanes.

But my job was demanding. I was always going on a trip somewhere. On this occasion it was to the West Indies. We were at Barbados Airport, Chapman and I, waiting to embark on the evening flight to Kingstown. Chapman said, "You didn't know X, who went down in the crash of a small plane in the Sudan? He's the only man I've known who carried his own chamber pot with him wherever he went. Not that there are no accidents here. Just last year the island beauty queen went down when the Guyanese pilot tried three times to land at Barbados in a rain storm. My own fear of flying goes back to the days when I had to take the Sikorsky flying boat from Georgetown to Port of Spain to catch the Royal Mail Lines boat. Those were wild takeoffs from the Demerara River, swerving to avoid floating tree trunks, the muddy water covering the port holes, almost submerging the hull."

St. Vincent is a rugged island, fertile and cloudy, its roads lined with the shiny-leaved breadfruit tree and the dark-leaved mango. Dorpfeld (my other colleague on this trip) came to life. "This's like Switzerland with bananas! I sink we do a lot here, no?"

"Bananas are our chief crop," confirmed the Chief Agricultural Officer (CAO). "Come into their own, they have. Shape was against them before. *Too suggestive.* Every week the banana boat go to Englan'. They pay double the world price. Well, we helped them in the War." [Helped us in the War? I never saw a banana. And all along my mother told us, "When we win the

War, you'll get to eat bananas – what a treat!" That explained it all, then: the buzz bombs, the troop convoys, the enemy submarines. It was a Banana War, a fierce one. Finally the banana ships came. Is this all there is to it? This bland thing?]

I took a day off to go to Bequia. At the dock was a small gaff-rigged Grenada-registered sloop, about thirty feet overall and eight in the beam. "Like the boat, white man? Farty t'ousand dollars and you take her!" But I was going to the Grenadines dock, to take passage on a rusty old freighter, the *Hairoun Star*, about to leave for Bequia. Soon after we embarked, a crew brought six amplifiers on board and placed them on the middle hatch. The switch was thrown and an enormous volume of sound came forth, something about a taxi in Grenada and a girl named Velma.

The beer flowed, the crew forgot to check the tickets and danced with the female passengers on deck. The *Hairoun Star* put to sea, listing to starboard, and an hour later noisily entered Admiralty Bay in Bequia, disturbing the peace of the yachts there. Once ashore I walked along the beach and encountered an old man building a boat. It was in frames. The stem and the sternpost were of natural-bent white cedar, felled on the island. The old man was beveling the ribs flush with the planked sides. "When I learned the trade," he told me, "I got paid fifty shillings a year, once a year, in arrears. The other lads said I was foolish. They got ready money fishing. Now the fish have gone."

After a lot of comic proceedings on St. Vincent – but this isn't the place to tell them – I boarded the plane to depart the island. A late-boarding passenger plunked down next to me. "Got to get out of these panty hose right away," she announced in a harsh New York accent. She reappeared from the rear toilet after a minute and sat down in the seat next to me. She ordered a large Scotch and fixed me with her eye. "Anyone who says a pilot is easy to live with is lying. I should know. I married one. Pride is their beset-ting sin. 'Hello, God,' I used to greet him. Pilots have lots of temptations, with all those good-looking stews. I should know. I was one. But I never messed around. Well, he found one that would. Met her in Japan. Thought he would start his own little harem. When I was through with him, he didn't own more than the clothes on his back. I singed that fly-boy's wings!"

I was in the ag department of Mega Bank for twelve years. I went on dozens of jaunts to weird places in the Middle East and the Caribbean countries. It would have taken a Robert Byron to do justice to the exquisite and exuberant humbug of it all.

17

IN THE COUNTRY OF EUPHORIA
(OSHKOSH 1986)

In the early days, the Experimental Aircraft Association's convention was held at the Rockford Airport in Illinois, a half-hour from where I lived at the time (1960). (I have one of the low EAA membership numbers, #2540.) For the particular 1986 convention of which I write, I drove to Oshkosh, WI, from my home in Manassas, VA

August 1 neared, and 20,000 airplanes revved their engines and headed for Oshkosh and funneled into Wittman Field – a stream of airplanes old and new, big and little over the course of the week. "I was doing great," I overheard a pilot say, "four and a half hours out of New York – I started with five hours fuel – when my engine quit over Lake Winnebago, within sight of the airport. I put her into the water a thousand yards short of the shoreline and some boaters picked us up."

August 1 neared, and forty thousand campers converged on Oshkosh – license plates of all fifty states: Alaska, Maine, Florida, California, and – significantly – Missouri, the "Show Me" state. (Some Doubting Thomas who'd come to verify…the fact of flying machines?) And there were the Canadians: "I've got plenty of time for my hobbies," one of them told me, "seeing as I live three hundred miles north of Edmonton and work in the air conditioning business."

August 1 neared, and I abandoned the plan to fly my Maule airplane to Oshkosh. A big old Bermuda High had been sitting out over the Atlantic for weeks, pumping hot, moist air over Virginia and the southern states. It was sunny, and it was IFR (instrument conditions) – thick haze and scattered thunderstorms. "Robbie, throw the pup tent in the trunk of the car, and let's hit the road." Then it started to rain. As we drove onto the Pennsylvania 'Pike, a big Pontiac, "a grocery getter," with the Confederate flag in lieu of a front license plate, cut in front of us on the entrance ramp and then spun out on the first curve, sliding back toward us head on. We avoided him and got into the middle of a long-distance, 18-wheeler truck race. No state police were in sight. We passed a car on fire on the shoulder; later, another car, a Cadillac, blazing fiercely. Like they say, the biggest risk in flying is driving to the airport.

Beyond the Appalachians, we got into a big pool of cool, clear air, and stayed in it 'til our return. Now we were wheeling across Indiana. Waves of airplane consciousness radiated from Oshkosh. Even the high-powered WLS radio station in Chicago was talking airplanes instead of blasting away with their "Rockin' America" program. "Y'have to fly these new planes IFR," explained an excited caller, "'cause the CG is so far back." We got to Oshkosh at 12.30P the following day, the first day of the convention, just in time to miss Jim Bede's lecture, "Design Problems of Supersonic Home-builts." (Darn! I wanted to hear that.) We paid our entrance fee and pitched our tent near a Dakota tipi, a single piece of canvas wrapped around 25-foot poles, its seam secured with 12-inch dowels.

"Did the Indians use canvas?"
"Yes, after the buffalo hides were gone."

That night the rain came down heavily, and the press of vehicles churned the tenting fields into mud.

Saturday morning, sunny. Imagine Disneyland with a crowd ninety percent white males, predominantly middle-aged, roving restlessly in search of…what? Reinforcement for our individual, nutty schemes? Well, yes. And there were 250 technical seminars, 500 exhibits, 20,000 airplanes, and gurus and pundits too numerous to count, from whom to glean ideas. I mingled with the crowds, listened to the chatter.

Welcome to Oshkosh 1986 by Paul Poberezny. "We've got to simplify flying and make it more attractive and available to more people. Right now the volume of knowledge required is enough to make someone turn to a horse." (Whoa, Paul! Horses aren't simple, either, or I wouldn't have got thrown off so often.)

Steve Wittman was eighty-two years old at this time. A skinny guy in a check shirt, he could have been your friendly local hardware clerk. In fact, he was an air racer in the 'thirties, and airport manager of Oshkosh Airport for many years. He designed a number of race planes (one of them hangs in the National Air and Space Museum in Washington, D.C.), and a classic 1953 homebuilt design, the Tailwind (one of them hung from the roof of my barn). He said, "The aerodynamicists at the University of Mississippi wouldn't believe my little plane could cruise 165 mph at 70-percent power. I let them test it: they calibrated the airspeed indicator, removed the prop and towed me to twelve thousand feet. On the way down we recorded the speeds and rate of descent. It's equivalent to a wind tunnel test. They admitted I was right – even a little conservative."

"My new design— you can see it on the flight line, in row 31—was designed to take me and my wife non-stop from Ocala, Florida, where we live in the winter, to Oshkosh. I call it the Model O-O."

"It looks like a Super Tailwind," I said.

"Oh, no! It's a completely new design." If Wittman were asked to design a replacement for the Boeing 747, would it be tube-and-fabric and look like a Tailwind sized up a hundred times? (I'm just kidding.)

Of Bob Hoover, aerobatic pilot. "Did you see that guy Hoover? He checked his airplane out for forty-five minutes before he went up. *Forty-five minutes!*"

Igor Bensen. We came upon Dr. Bensen – the disciple of Sikorsky and the designer of the gyrocopter – explicating in one of the red-and-blue striped forum tents. Despite his Russian accent and machine-gun delivery – he talked in short bursts – his audience was deeply absorbed. "Vertical control vehicles have unlimited potential. It would be very easy, for example, to convert a suitable family-sized vehicle, say a Jeep, to cross any type of terrain or river by means of a mechanism incorporating a balloon for ascent, a propeller for motion through the air, and a parachute to land. Very easy. Check out Santos-Dumont. He was doing this sort of thing in 1901, landing in the gardens of his friends in Paris." (Why not? Last year there was a man here from California with a pedal-powered blimp.)

Q. Will vertical flight become more important?
A. No. (Explanation extremely long, incomprehensible, and off the point, the whole illustrated with little chalk diagrams that cluttered the blackboard.)

Burt Rutan was down on the flight line, sitting on the grass next to one of his canard designs, surrounded by a circle of disciples and admirers. His brother Dick was elsewhere on the field. The next month, Dick was going to fly around the world non-stop. It was Burt's idea. "When Dick got out of the Air Force, he didn't have a job, so he went over to Mohave, and Burt gave him a job in his airplane factory. But Dick soon got in Burt's hair – Dick wouldn't do nothing useful, just wanted to test airplanes – so Burt said, 'Dick, why don't you go fly around the world. I'll design the plane, and you take the project from there.' That was five years ago. Then Dick decided the co-pilot should be his girlfriend, Jeanna. 'No girlfriend,' decreed brother Burt. But what with the fourteen gas tanks, and the feeder tank, and Dick's sideburns and cowboy boots, there wasn't room for anything but a very small co-pilot. So Burt relented on the girl." (Never mind the scuttlebutt; Rutan and Yeager made their great flight in December 1986. For a definitive account, see *The First Unrefueled Flight Around the World*, by Richard Taylor, 1994.)

Jim Bede. We missed his first forum (the one on supersonic homebuilts), and he didn't show up for the second. Jim was conspicuous by his absence. But in his days of glory, before his business collapsed, Jim was No.1 personality in the amateur airplane builder's world. A corpulent figure in a red jumpsuit and matching red hat, sometimes mistaken by the uninitiated for a Coca-Cola delivery man, Jim had dreams to sell, potent dreams. I first heard about the BD-5 in 1970, when several Chapter 86 members put down deposits for kit packages from Bede Aircraft. (The gory details are available on *Wikipedia*.) Now, in 1986, Jim was a Personality. Hadn't his jet airplane design, the BD-5J, featured in the opening sequence of the film *Octopussy*, outstanding cultural event of the known world?

I asked a man from NASA about the BD5 and took down what I thought he said. "It's really a good design concept, though it's difficult to build and tricky to fly. It looks like it flies a lot faster than 200 mph, because it's small like a bullet. Eleven thousand orders were taken for kits, 55 were completed, and twenty pilots killed so far. It's a nice design, though the narrow-chord wing operates at a Reynolds number of about one million, so it sacrifices some lift. It's not so hard to fly except for pilot-induced oscillation. Of course, with that high thrust-line, she'll pitch up if you lose power – that's a killer. The jet version is *sweet* to fly, though I got G-lock on two occasions. But I love the BD-5."

Dave Blanton, a peppery man from Wichita, held forth on Auto Engine Development: "I told Rutan, 'It's stupid to fly around the world with an air-cooled engine.'" Then Dave got going on the Ford V-6 aluminum engine. [Robbie: "Dad, that's the engine we've got in our car!"] "Change the camshaft to move maximum torque to 4400 RPM; junk the EPA package; junk the stock carburetor and replace it with a two-barrel 500 cfm Holley carb. The Holley's a good one, though their legal department is a bunch of idiot fools. Then put on a 2:1 belt-driven reduction gear [Dave sells this], and you're ready to go."

Q. What about foreign engines?
A. I won't work on them.
Q. What about fuel injection?
A. Unreliable.

Q. What about diesel engines?

A. Too exotic.

Q. Do you like oil treatments?

A. No.

Q. Can I port the intakes?

A. This is America. Do as you damn well please.

Q. Where do you get your power figures?

A. I use a dynamometer on everything.

"He never even seen a dynamometer," said Beachner, who flew a Buick-engined homebuilt, until it quit on him and he was killed later in the week. (I was sorry for that.)

A giddy feeling was engendered in the thronging crowds from all the possibilities.

Duane Cole, dean of aerobatics: "I can list you pages of people who have killed themselves at air shows – flying too low, attempting maneuvers beyond their ability, and flying too low. I fly *higher* than anyone else. And I've flown *longer* than anyone else. Think about it! There are only 220,000 general aviation aircraft in this country, and we lose 1,000 pilots a year. (Plaintively) When are guys going to look out for themselves?"

At 12.30A on the third night, I was awakened by voices outside the tent. It was Bill Cahill and Joe Schweitzer, my ancient companions and backyard airplane builders. "Can you get us in on your pass?" "Sure." I left Robbie asleep in the tent and went off with them to the parking lot, to Joe's truck. We reminisced, drank two six-packs of beer between us – and forgot all about getting Joe's truck into the camp grounds. Bill said, "Witherspoon has been a student pilot for thirty years. By trade he's a parts man. He has a remarkable head for numbers. It's really a shame clouds don't have parts numbers."

"Joe, what is this switch on the steering wheel?"

It's the solenoid switch on my fuel transfer system," said Joe. "With four tanks, I can drive non-stop from Chicago to Ogallala. I'm testing the system before putting it in my plane. Don't forget, if you get lost in the air, you are going to need extra fuel. Like when I was a crew member flying in a B-36 over the Pacific. Eventually we got lost. So we flew around until we spotted a ship and asked for her position."

Dawn was breaking; aero engines revved on the field. A flight of four P-51s took off and flew over the camp ground, over the 655 portable toilets, the 256 pay-phones, the 200 shower units, the 40,000 campers, and the 20,000 airplanes.

Workshops galore. Welding guru showing tyro how to weld chrome moly tube: "Let the puddle melt the rod!" Aside: "God! It's so simple. You'd think I was teaching him how to do a slow roll."

Tent No. 9 was where the FAA gave non-stop sermons on flight safety. I listened spellbound to an Elmer Gantry who recounted blood-curdling stories, true and tragic tales, of rash printers, foolish paper-mill operatives, and fledgling mechanics who launched into the air in the face of every principle of airmanship. "The airport operator pleaded with him not to take off, but he flew away in the fog and crashed within seconds." And to what avail, these sermons? After the flying displays were over, and the air space was free, a big thundercloud drifted over the airfield, crackling forked lightning from its base. Pilots forgot the lectures on micro-bursts, forgot about prudence altogether. Still giddy from all the things they'd seen and heard at this convention, they jumped into their airplanes and rose joyfully into the air: columns of airplanes – warbirds and ultralights – rose up from Whitman Field toward the dark underside of the thunder cloud, like metal filings to a magnet, like sinners to sin. Said Robbie, "If we get hail, it'll take out half of general aviation in the United States!" But the storm drifted off and dumped seven inches of rain on Milwaukee.

Airframes and Engines. "Bill," I said, "how do you suppose I can inspect the insides of my Tailwind's wings for rot?" "The best advice I can give to you is to take a match and burn 'em," growled Bill. "I wouldn't mess with wooden structures over ten years old. And I trust wooden construction more than amateur welding – or composites. Or metal, come to that. You'll remember Al took me up in his T-18 that morning, and it fell apart in the air that same afternoon."

"Don't forget engines," chimed in Bob Polaski. "You remember Jim Daniel's Volksplane?" [I did remember it.] "He sold it to a guy I knew. Soon after he got the plane, the new owner didn't return from a local flight. The CAP was called out. I went up in my [Cessna] one-fifty to help out. It isn't easy to spot a downed plane from the air, but I found it in the corn. When we reached him he was dead in the cockpit, almost within sight of a farmer mowing his yard. That pilot had survived two years flying gunships in Nam. I don't know why it crashed but I blame the Volkswagon engine – they don't belong in airplanes."

"The most beautiful sound I ever heard was a twelve cylinder Jag," said someone, *a propos* of nothing. "It sounded like ripping silk."

Best of the Flying Displays: The Harrier, in perfect hovering flight, and able to rotate about its vertical axis. The Helio, a fixed-wing airplane that can land in one hundred feet. A Boeing 747 flying by on one engine – the other three shut down – and climbing away!

Robbie and I stayed seven days at the convention. When we drove back to Virginia I found myself fixating on....gyrocopters – whirling along under that free-spinning rotor, landing in my own backfield, parking next to the tractor.

18

UPS AND DOWNS

Sometime in 1987 Helen upset my complacency by announcing she planned to leave me – and the kids – in the East while she made a new life on the Pacific Coast. She'd had enough of commuting to work, of my airplanes, and Mega Bank, too. "I could have screamed while you prattled on about "easy living" she explained.

I quit the bank at the end of September. (A move made easier by a windfall gain from a real estate sale.) Then I saw an advertisement in the Washington *Post*: "Eastern shore of Virginia: colonial house on deep-water dock." In January 1988 I flew a Cessna 150 across the Chesapeake Bay to the house with the deep water dock (saw that it was frequented by otters, ospreys, and eagles) and moved there the following June with Phyllis (Robbie was in Alaska.) It was hot weather, the movers (those recruited in Onancock) were mostly drunk. ("Where shall I put the snow shoes?")

Meanwhile, to sharpen my flying skills, I used some "retraining" money from my erstwhile employer to renew my commercial pilot license and instrument rating at Manassas Airport; an enjoyable boondoggle. I divided 200 hours between instrument approaches to area airports in a Piper Warrior, and maneuvers such as chandelles, steep spirals and "eights around pylons" in a Piper Arrow. It was fun. "A commercial pilot license won't get you very far," said my instructor, patronizingly. (But Chuck, I don't want a job. I just want to improve my skills as a pleasure pilot...)

In the spring of 1988 I had some lawyer business in Miami, so I flew there from Manassas on a training flight with my instructor in a Turbo Arrow. (It was 6.7 hours, with a re-fueling stop at Charleston, SC.) I flew the airplane off the Manassas runway in full IFR while Chuck handled the radios and, when things settled down, regaled me with an account of his exploits with various girlfriends. From Charleston we were vectored way out over the Atlantic to avoid coastal storms. After a stay in downtown Miami (near to where the flying boat leaves for the Islands) we drove to the airport. But where was it? No one on the streets could tell us. They spoke only Spanish.

Flying back to Manassas over the coastal plain, in excellent visibility, I was impressed by the tedium of "flying the airways." There's little to see from ten thousand feet, and compulsory reporting interrupted my reveries. (Chuck was "eating it up", building his hours.)

The air traveler sees everything and nothing. I love the wide views. But I want to know that Sioux Falls is more than just a place at the intersection of two interstate highways with an aerial view of some big, blocky meat packing plants and a penitentiary with guard towers. I want to get down close and see the multitude of taverns, the clock tower in mock Venetian style; I want to smell the shopping mall with its ghastly perfumed air conditioning. I want to go into the pungent stock yards and see a ten-year-old boy spitting in the dirt, just like his father.

In March 1988, I interrupted my flying course at Manassas to attend an eight-day "wave camp" at California City, a world record site for soaring. (Before I went, I practiced with a dozen glider flights at Front Royal, VA.) There was just one "wave day" at the camp – and one opportunity to soar in the lee of the Sierras. That was on the sixth day, on March 15. We got the call early: "Get to the airport right away!" Not everyone had flown in a wave, and preferred to go with an instructor. But I had flown at Colorado Springs, years before, in the lee of Pikes Peak. So I said I was ready to go, and was first or second off. It was a wild ride, that tow, requiring full deflections of the controls to keep upright. After release, I entered a downdraft and headed toward the desert floor and the nasty-looking mesquite. A quick turn took me back into the wave and once there, in the powerful wave, it was smooth flying. I rapidly gained 14,500 feet, flying into the wind, matching my flying speed to the wind speed to hold position over the ground. But at 20,000 feet I broke off – because I wasn't confident I understood the oxygen system in this particular airplane, a G103, though I'd had plenty of time to learn it. (No excuse for that.) I arrived back over California City at 12,000 feet (9,500 ft AGL) and made a straight ahead descent with dive brakes out, into the strong wind. The entire flight lasted 1.3 hours. This one flight was worth going all the way to California. It was my one hundredth glider flight.

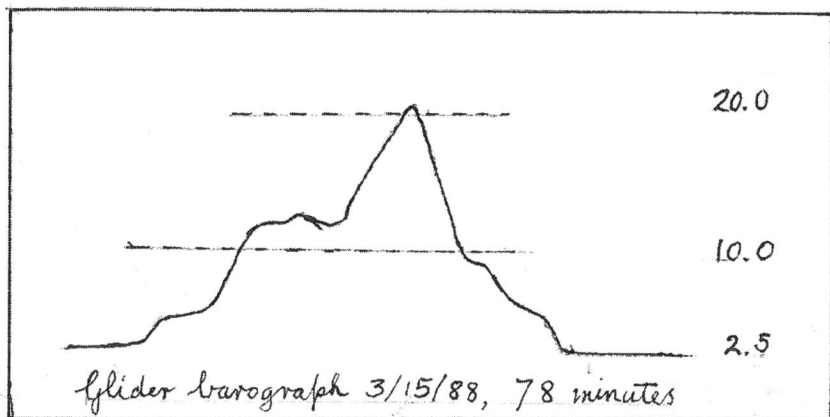

glider barograph 3/15/88, 78 minutes

G-103 sailplane barograph California City, 3/15/88, California City elevation 2,454 ft. Release 5,500 ft, high point 20,000 ft plus.

Ch. 19. With Doug Schultz (R), my instructor on the P-51, Kissimmee, FL, 1989. Doug was killed flying a MIG 21, 1999.

19

MAKING OUT WITH
THE MUSTANG

I was in need of a fillip: I'd go fly a Mustang. What is it about WW2 airplanes? They are names associated with potency, speed and combat. Some say that the older prop planes are more glamorous, more available, and – up to a point – more manageable than the jets. But this is a matter of degree. At the deepest level, why do some persons need to fly an airplane, gallop a horse, or shoot skeet; while others like working crossword puzzles? What's this presumed primacy of the physical, over pondering – cogitating – meditating? Because the physical world is trumps, that's why.

Fifty years after the war, only a few hundred aircraft remained of the hundreds of thousands manufactured. Only two hundred P-51s and 500 Texan trainers remained in the USA, along with a scattering of contemporary WW2 aircraft elsewhere. To fly one of these obsolete aircraft, while managing the torque from its big propeller and the ground-looping proclivities of its tail-wheel landing gear, is a special experience. These are complex machines, with associated noise, smell of oil, G-force and lots of glamour. From its introduction, the 51 was notable for its laminar wing and huge fuel capacity. Range with drop tanks was 2,055 miles. Expect to find more pages in the pilot's handbook devoted to fuel management than to flying the airplane.

Of course, you can't get into one of these airplanes with a private pilot's license and expect to fly it away. Minimum preparation for conversion training is a rating to commercial standards in a plane equipped with retractable gear and constant speed propeller, as well as plenty of tail-dragger time, preferably one hundred hours in an AT-6. As I had these qualifications, I applied to Kissimmee, FL to take instruction in P-51 Mustang airplane, N851D, a D model modified to carry a second pilot in tandem. This airplane was operated by Stallion 51 Corporation, owned by Doug Schultz, a Delta Airlines pilot, and Lee Lauderback, corporate pilot for Arnold Palmer. N851D was powered by a 2,000 HP Rolls-Royce engine. All-up weight was 8,000 lbs. Instruction cost $1,500 per hour (1989).

I took thirteen hours of instruction over three days in May 1989 in N851D. The course was comprehensive, and painstaking in detail. It was hard work. It included fifty touch-and-goes and much else. After a thorough preliminary briefing I was ready for the first take-off. I felt confident with that wide track landing gear and in following the instructions for take-off: seven degrees of right rudder trim and smooth initial application of power to 32 inches before feeding in the remainder. (With the tremendous torque of this engine-propeller combination, mishandling of the throttle – say, on go-around – could turn the airplane upside down.) The landing pattern involves a continuous shallow banking turn. An overhead entry to the landing pattern is initiated by approaching the runway at 200 knots, two hundred feet above pattern height, losing speed on the initial turn-in by pulling some G and cutting the power back. Whoopee! On the final approach, the student needs to keep the same rate of descent such that all necessary adjustments are made ten seconds from touching down at 95-100 kts.

My instructor was Doug Schultz. (Doug died in 1999, in the crash of a MIG-21, Mach 2 fighter.) The entries he wrote in my log book were as follows: "Preflight, normal and emergency procedures, systems. Take-off, turns, steep turns, & reversals. Clean/dirty slow flight. Clean & dirty stalls, accelerated stalls. Buffet maneuv, aileron/barrel rolls, wingovers. Loops, 1/2 Cuban 8's, Immelmans, Clover leafs up & down. Unusual attitudes, dynamic-performance maneuvers. Lift vector turns. Departure turns, low-level maneuv, sim. engine failure. Approach/ldg, overhead and downwind pattern entries, 50 T & G landings, 9 full-stop ldgs, 5 go-arounds, 30-deg X-wind ldgs. One RT & one Left fully-developed progressive spins, Split-S's."

I felt queasy with all this G force, but I only threw up once, into a bag.

With this check-out, I got the endorsement "found qualified to pilot the P-51." I'd "made out with the Mustang," but it was a relationship unconsummated by solo flight. To have soloed the plane, I would have had to buy her. I would, too, if I had had a spare million.

Ch. 19. "O for a life of sensations rather than of thoughts." (John Keats)
Author in the driver's seat of P-51 at Kissimmee, FL, May 1989.

Ch. 20. 1946 Cessna 140 on EDO 1650 floats; 0-290 engine. Back River, MD, 1990. "They can't build a better airplane now than they did in 1946." The two floats support twice the loaded weight of the seaplane. Scott handling the bow lines, engine off. With the prop spinning, he turned his back on me, and I feared his decapitation. I flew this airplane solo, coast-to-coast, taking the route of the first crossing of North America by Alexander Mackenzie in 1792-93, following seventeen Canadian rivers and crossing a score of lakes. High winds in the interior of the country and fog on the coast kept me grounded for days, making for a slow, thirty-day trip.

20

FLYING A FLOATPLANE

In 1974 I bought plans for 1200-size floats from a designer in Quebec with the idea of converting the Fly Baby to floats and flying her to Canada – a project I had to defer.) Now it looked like I'd have the chance to follow through with floatplane flying. While flying from Manassas in1987 I learned from a chance conversation about the seaplane base at Baltimore. I followed this up and found I could learn to fly a floatplane there – a six-hour course of flight instruction – in Mike Forster's Aeronca Chief fitted with 1400-size floats.

Baltimore is home to the only seaplane base for miles around, located just east of the city on Back River, a place frequented by herons and ospreys. From its sandy beach, which adjoins an air strip, you can sometimes see seaplanes being launched on to the river, which is very wide at this point. Here I would learn the rudiments of flying a seaplane, splashing around on Back River, with occasional side trips to the nearby Severn River at Annapolis.

I arrived at Back River that bright morning in October, 1988, and came upon the Aeronca seaplane parked on the grass in front of the flight office, about five hundred yards from the river. An ungainly little beast, this little airplane with enormous "boots", as ungainly as only a specialized creature – a camel or a stork – can be. Then Mike Forster showed up, and the course began. Once in the cockpit I saw there was very little difference from the landplane version of this machine. The water rudder on the end of the starboard pontoon was operated by the same rudder bar which worked the air rudder. Six hours of instruction, I supposed, quite incorrectly, would be ample for such a simple craft. And then…well, here it all was: the seaplane, the river, and – to the west – all of North America.

"Do you know how to handle a sailboat?
"Yes."
"It's something like that." (But not much, I was to discover.)

Mike went to the hangar behind the flight office, and came back with two helpers and four iron pipes (troublesome pipes, as I would find out later). We were going to load the seaplane on to a trailer which was then to be towed by tractor down to the beach. Not as awkward as transporting a baby whale, the procedure consisted, basically, of backing the trailer up to the seaplane, placing the iron pipes crosswise on the bed of the trailer, then depressing the rear of the trailer while pushing down on the rear end of the floats (to elevate the bows) and – here came the tricky part – pushing the seaplane up the incline of the trailer to roll forward over the wobbling iron pipes. Once at the beach, the trailer would be backed into the water, the lines loosed from the bow cleats, and the plane allowed to float free – to bob on the water, to come alive.

"One thing about seaplanes," said Mike, "You're very dependent on other people."

This did not seem to bother Mike. Benign of manner, prematurely white-haired (his flying career had included dodging SAM missiles over Hanoi), Mike had graduated from the Naval Academy at Annapolis in the 1950s and now – the apple had not fallen far from the tree – he operated a seaplane school on Back River.

No windsock was visible from the beach, and there were no buoys to mark a runway on the water. The only markers, such as the red triangle on a stake at the end of the sand spit called Witchcoat Point, were intended for boat navigation. Just then a visiting seaplane landed out in the river beyond this point and taxied back towards us on the beach. The seaplane pilot didn't see the marker and plowed across the sand spit, which was under a few inches of water at the current state of the tide, with only a momentary shudder of the airplane. "He could have ripped the floats off," I suggested. "That's why seaplane insurance is so high," said Mike. But he seemed more interested in the Chesapeake Bay Retriever that was seated next to the pilot of the incoming seaplane.

Which direction should we use for takeoff? I looked at the smokestacks on Sparrows Point but couldn't tell within a wide arc where the wind was coming from. I pulled up a handful of grass and threw it into the air. The wind was southeast. By taking up seaplaning I was reverting to the early practices of flying, when airplanes, like swans – or storks – took off and landed directly into wind. Mike hand-cranked the prop (from the rear, standing on the right float) to start the engine and then we taxied out into the middle of the river. Mike said, "Here's how to tell where the wind's coming from." He retracted the water rudder, and the little seaplane, lacking any keel, weathercocked smartly into the wind.

"Let's take off," said Mike.

I pushed the throttle wide and started the seaplane, engine snarling, across the water. I have flown little airplanes that practically jumped into the air. But this strange machine simply plowed through the water, shook and vibrated, threw up clouds of spray – and remained glued to the water. "The shore is coming up," I yelled at Mike, above the engine noise and the rush of water. "Hold her down," he said. The plane picked up a little more speed; then, when Mike motioned me to relax the forward pressure on the yoke, the plane unstuck from the water and climbed slowly, marvelously, above the river bank.

"Seaplanes need *twice* the distance to take off," yelled Mike, echoing Anne Morrow Lindbergh's *Listen! The Wind*.

We circled and descended to the river. "See those wind streaks on the water?" said Mike. By then, the engine was throttled back so it was easy to talk. The wind streaks were not aligned with our flight path. The wind had changed direction, and I was drifting sideways down to the water.

"See what I mean!" he said. We veered away from the water and made a fresh approach.

In these training sessions, during four days in October, we practiced three dozen takeoffs and landings, and other acts of buoyancy besides – bouncing, leaping, splashing on and off the nearby rivers. On one occasion we beached the seaplane at a riverside restaurant across the Bay to eat our lunch. Flying, floating, I rejoiced in these maneuvers, freed from the constraining boundaries of the land.

The final part of the seaplane curriculum (or arcanum, as I now thought of it) was "sailing." Sailing is the technique of reaching a desired point on a beach or dock in conditions of high wind, especially on a lee shore. Unlike a sailboat, a floatplane cannot move crosswind in such conditions – the windward wing wants to tip up and dunk the airplane. The solution is to reach the beach by drifting the craft backward, looking over one's shoulder for reference, while keeping the seaplane headed into the wind (water rudder retracted), with engine on to control rate of backward drift. But the usable part of the beach at Back River Seaplane Base is fairly small and, with the wind blowing onshore, it is a nice trick to track backwards to the desired spot on the beach. At first I would end up a hundred yards from my objective and have to motor out into the river and try again. In such conditions the small seaplane demonstrated its essential unhandiness and revealed the need for yet-to-be-acquired skills to master her. Those skills, I realized, would have to be acquired "on the job," flying coast to coast. (Luck, I began to see, would be a big part of it, too. Long-distance flyer Francis Chichester, who attempted to fly his Moth seaplane around the world, characterized small seaplanes as "about as seaworthy as a canoe.")

After my final lesson with Mike, I took the rating check with the examiner. That done, I hosed down the Aeronca with fresh water and drove back to my house across the Bay. From Back River to the Bay Bridge at Annapolis takes ten minutes in a slow plane, but can take sixty to ninety minutes by car, in among ten thousand other cars crawling along the road like so many cockroaches. I thought about the directness of flying, and I thought about the view I was missing from the ground – that from only four hundred feet above road level, the field of vision would be a hundred times enlarged. Still preoccupied with the pleasures of flying, I drove across the Bay Bridge and looked without enthusiasm at the boats, which on the Chesapeake are all too often – if they have any sort of draft – confined to narrow, marked channels and lack the freedom of an airplane to take any path its pilot chooses.

Early in the spring of 1989, I began looking for a seaplane to buy. Two or three dozen used seaplanes were listed for sale in *Trade-A-Plane*, the yellow aviation trade paper that covers the entire country. I ran down each of these leads, telephoning New York, Florida, Massachusetts, Maine, Minnesota, and Tennessee. There was a likely sounding Cessna for sale in Maine, a Type 172, with a low-time engine. But the owner had sold the floats separately before I called. And "Greg," in Minnesota, had changed his mind about selling his plane: "...the float package is too hard to come by."

The last of these ads was for a 1946 Cessna, Model 140, with a 135 HP engine and extra fuel tanks. I went to Chattanooga to see this airplane, and found her in good shape, so I bought her. She was mounted on two EDO aluminum floats, each about fourteen feet long, with a "step" on the keel about halfway back to break the suction on takeoff. The fuselage was of aluminum too, but the wings were fabric-covered ("rag wings") – fabric is not only lighter than metal but also safer. (Periodic replacement of the fabric will show up any corrosion of the aluminum wing spars.) Best of all, perhaps, this airplane carried a non-standard fifty gallons of gas in four wing tanks and had a range in still air of 575 miles.

This buoyant craft had 167 square feet of wing to lift her, to fly her 1,650 pounds loaded weight around the sky, and a generous 3,300 pounds of flotation in her two pontoons to hold her high on the water. (Whence these specifications? An empirical process, no doubt, learned from the trials and tribulations of ancestral seaplanes.)

When I bought her, the little Cessna seaplane was based at Lake Chickamauga on the Tennessee River. It was a long way back to Baltimore in a slow airplane, more than a day's flying I figured, as I anticipated going round the bottom of the Appalachian range instead of flying directly across those mountains. I could expect to get to Norfolk by the end of the first day, but not in one hop. I could land at any one of the boat marinas along the way, but they would be congested because of the Memorial Day Holiday. And I did not relish the prospect of a collision with a boat or jetty – or any encounter with boaters who did not know that a seaplane is as fragile as a carton of eggs. Only one suitable landing place on my route was listed in the seaplane directory: Piedmont Bible College, in Mocksville, North Carolina. I telephoned the office. "Come on in," I was told; then, by way of apology or explanation, "It's only a pond." (See Map in appendix.)

My newly acquired airplane had neither communications radio nor radio-direction finder, only a magnetic compass. On May 29, 1989, I took off from Lake Chickamauga in hazy weather and headed southeast, to go round the bottom of the Appalachians before turning northeast to Mocksville. The compass needle spun erratically in its housing. (Later, someone noticed that there was no kerosene in the housing to dampen the vibration.) The tops of the mountains were in clouds, and I stayed low and followed the line of foothills as a seaman might follow a strange coast, as Amerigo Vespucci coasted the eastern seaboard of America. I went around the bottom of the mountain chain, turned northeast, and flew parallel with the near ridge, but tentatively, like a tiercel's first migration. I was headed over country I'd never traveled, toward landing areas I didn't know, in a machine in which I could barely claim competency – a delicious feeling of adventure.

After fifty minutes I flew past a water tower with a name painted on the tank: TOCCOA, GA, a town across the Georgia line from South Carolina. As I flew on, jubilant, to the northeast, the sky gradually cleared. I flew low over Greensboro, NC, looking down on its streets and buildings and at the lines streaming back from the bow cleats on my airplane's floats. I found the pond at the Bible College without much trouble (there is an adjoining airstrip clearly visible from the air), and I circled the still pond and saw a man and a boy fishing off a pier. I buzzed the airstrip to let the duty personnel know I had arrived, then splashed down on to the pond too fast, doing "ducks and drakes," like a flat stone skipping across the water. A man, who proved to be the chief instructor, came down to the pond and directed me by hand signals to a beach. There he refueled my seaplane from a gas truck and pumped water out of my floats.

Prominent in the flight office was a wall map of Brazil, where the school sends a quota of missionaries after the chief instructor has taught them to fly. That was his purpose. What was mine? he asked.

"To fly to the Pacific," I told him. "I'm following the route of Alexander Mackenzie." (Who?)

"I flew a Super Cub all the way from Alaska," he told me, "but it flipped over on the lake here during a training flight. It's in the hangar there, wrecked." (An engaging thought: if a plane can crash with the chief instructor aboard, then there's no shame to a novice having a crackup or two.)

I started the engine and taxied out on the pond for takeoff. The "pond" was smaller than the extensive stretches of water at Back River and Lake Chickamauga; moreover, my plane was fitted with a coarse-pitch propeller (fifty inches of pitch), which favored cruise flight at the expense of takeoff and climb (forty inches of pitch for this engine). Nor was there any headwind to help shorten the takeoff run. All was still. I taxied to the very edge of the pond, lowered the flaps twenty degrees, and retracted the water rudder. I looked back at the Bible College, and then to the heavens for any sign of wind. Within seconds a headwind rippled the water.

As I readied the plane for takeoff, I felt a familiar rush of adrenaline, just as when I was steeplechasing, taking a fence. I would check the horse's speed, steady him, and – on the right stride – ease off on the reins, and put in the spur to launch him into the air. (It was "neck or nothing." Sometimes I came a cropper.) Now, looking across the pond, I opened the throttle, plowed across the water, and got the floats onto the "step." As the far shore came up, I tugged back on the yoke to pull the plane off the water – but prematurely – and this action submerged the rear end of the floats and slowed me down. I pushed the yoke forward, built up some more speed, then tried again. Same result. To the watchers on the shore – the chief instructor, the man and the boy fishing off the pier – my takeoff must have resembled that of a cormorant, when its webbed feet drag the water in a series of splashes. Finally I succeeded in pulling the seaplane off the water and over the dam at the end of the pond, barely clearing the trees. Release from the water's grip provoked a surge of exultation, a random snatch of song as I flew away into the clear blue sky toward the northeast. (Like Chichester, I was exhilarated, "half intoxicated," with floatplane flying, which left "the once considered marvel of landplane flying a dull old show.") With float flying, I recaptured my first heady days in the air: a peculiar mixture of novelty, exultation, and over-reaching – call it euphoria – which is like falling in love.

Little more than an hour elapsed before I came to another water tower, HENDERSON, N.C. This was good progress. Why not skip Norfolk and its unfamiliar landing area and go on to Baltimore? Why not? I was free as a bird. All I had to do was to figure my remaining fuel ("don't rely on the gauges!"), pencil in a thick black line on the chart direct to Baltimore, then alter heading to fly that line of flight. Soon I saw the office towers of Richmond miles ahead, incongruous in the surrounding "bush." Then I passed low, yet lofty, over seven rivers – the James, York, Rappahannock, Potomac, Patuxent, Severn, Patapsco – that flow into the Chesapeake, and finally arrived over Back River, the surface of which was chopped up by the wind. I buzzed the adjoining airstrip and caught Mike Forster, to whom I had not given advance notice of my arrival, just as he was leaving for home. He and his helpers came down to the beach and pulled my seaplane out of the water. This, an eight-hour trip, was my first solo flight in a seaplane.

21

BEHIND THE EIGHT BALL

Item: Watch the Prop!

While readying the plane for its trans-Canada flight, I made periodic test hops from Back River. After one of these flights, Mike's helper, Scott, almost lost his head. When I taxied up to the beach, I saw that Scott had backed the trailer into the river and was waiting for me to drive the seaplane onto it, as onto a ramp. When I was thirty feet away, Scott, who was standing on the trailer just above the waterline, turned his back on me to talk to a bystander. I yanked the throttle right back to slow the seaplane, but she had way on her, and kept going, propeller whirring, toward Scott on the trailer. I shouted at him; there was no response. The seaplane kept on, propeller whirring. In a panic I yelled, "GET OFF THE TRAILER!" He was absorbed in conversation and couldn't hear me over the engine noise. The seaplane approached the near end of the trailer. Scott's decapitation was imminent. Who would tell his mother?

I cut the ignition. The propeller slowed and stopped. The seaplane, losing way, slued around into wind and broadsided the tires of the trailer, then drifted away. Scott looked complacently around, waded into the water, took hold of the grab line attached to the bow cleat of the near float, and pulled the plane back to the trailer.

Drained by this experience, I stopped at the first lounge on the road home to top up on a couple of sixty-cent beers. There were about forty patrons at the bar, attended by three television sets and two of what were surely the biggest and homeliest barmaids in America. Not one of the patrons wasted his time watching the TV or the barmaids, but each busied himself with his drinking buddies and his beer. A latecomer who attempted some banter with one of the barmaids – he tried to hurry her along – was ejected.

Item: Slipping, Skidding

Look up and see, any time of day or night, an airplane overhead, flying through the air like a car driving along a road. How can the layman know that flight is a balancing act of opposing forces acting upon the airplane? (Why should he care?)

When floats (pontoons) are attached to a landplane, the extra side area of the floats that is ahead of the turning axis of the airplane reduces the effect of the tail. Like an ill-fashioned wind vane, the airplane may set crabwise relative to its passage through the air. At slow speeds in this condition, especially in a turn, one wing could lose lift, and the plane flip over in a stall and spin. (Let me not be tempted to exaggerate the instability of my seaplane; it was no Sopwith Camel, and none of my test flights came close to V.M. Yeates' hair-raising account of his first solo flight at Croydon in a Sopwith Camel, as related in his uber-literate account *Winged Victory*.)

To counter this condition of skidding or slipping flight without the auxiliary fins of Mike's Aeronca, my seaplane needed continuous correction from the rudder. But which rudder pedal to push I could best determine if I knew the direction of the relative wind. My first thought was to attach a tuft of wool, with tape, to the center of the front windshield, an idea borrowed from glider pilots, who had adapted the "telltale" used on the front or backstay of a sailboat to detect this relative wind. But surely water spray would loosen any tape applied to the windshield? So I attached an inclinometer, with two machine screws, to the cockpit dash.

This instrument, introduced in the 1930s, looks something like a carpenter's level. The curved glass tube contains kerosene and a steel ball bearing, which is free to move in the tube. Normally the ball rests at the bottom of the curved tube, but with any unbalanced force, such as slip or skid, the ball moves in the direction of that force. The old-timers, who weren't, perhaps, such seat-of-the-pants fliers as they claimed, kept an eye on this ball and kicked in left or right rudder as necessary to keep it centered. That's all there is to it.

Item: Weigh Airplane

> *In this slender vessel, we shipped provisions, goods for presents, arms, ammunition, and baggage, to the weight of three thousand pounds, and an equipage of ten people.* (Mackenzie, *Voyages.*)

I, too, expected to carry a load of gear on my trip across North America. And that gear would have to be loaded properly. Flying an airplane with the center of gravity too far aft because of an unbalanced load is, at best, dicey. But where were the plane's weight and balance computations? Gone astray. As soon as I could, I rented two Fairbanks-Morse scales, each rated at 1,000 pounds, and enlisted Mike Forster and his helpers to manhandle the scales, one under each float. The sum of the two readings was 1,105 pounds, very close to Chichester's Moth seaplane. Then, to determine the center of gravity of my Cessna seaplane, we removed the scales and balanced her on a two-inch pipe, placed under the pontoons at the point where the plane would teeter either forward or backwards, like a see-saw.

A bystander: "They can't build a better plane now than they did in 1946!" It was true. My seaplane looked good: all compound curves – a pretty thing, a bathing beauty, an elegant toy. (And not so long ago, I had characterized floatplanes as misshapen storks!)

We measured the distance back from the wing's leading edge (the datum) to the plane's point of balance: 14.7 inches. These figures – the airplane's empty weight and the location of its point of balance – I entered in the airplane log. With this information, I was able to compute how much of my gear could be safely stowed in the baggage compartment behind the seats, and how much would have to come forward to be strapped to the passenger seat beside me.

Item: Get a Radio

One cold, gray – but promising – day in November, I drove over the Key Bridge in Baltimore to Martin Airport on Middle River to see about getting a radio installed in my plane. The sky was leaden, and the waters of Baltimore Harbor a sickly yellow-green-gray color, whipped up to bobbing white horses by the wind. I drove up to the airport and walked into the cavernous, well heated hangars filled with corporate planes whose polished aluminum skins reflected the light from a multitude of overhead fluorescent lamps. (Significant to me is that this is the place where Martin built the China Clippers – big, beautiful flying boats that inaugurated Pan Am's routes to the Orient in 1935.)

I looked for the radio shop, missed my way, and stopped in a dingy back office, where I encountered an old man with rheumy eyes sitting at a battered sewing machine. "Before the war," he said, without any prompting, "I was a tailor, and during the war I had sixty-six people working under me – fifty-three women and thirteen men – doing the upholstery on the bombers. This plant turned out one B-26 every four hours. If Hitler only knew! Twenty-four hours a day, seven days a week – that was the schedule. But people were different then."

The warrior-tailor directed me to the radio shop, where I found half-a-dozen technicians, seemingly without tasks (maybe it was their lunch hour?). No-one could answer my questions, or knew whether they could service a seaplane at Back River. (I never did get a radio installed, but later bought a hand-held transceiver instead.)

Item: Patch the Float

I drove to Back River as often as I could and worked on my list of "items to be done." In the course of this work I suffered through the whole range of body contortions associated with groping in the wing roots (where I installed two aerials, one in each wing), as well as the baggage compartment, under the instrument panel, and inside a float. For there was now a hole in the right float. It happened this way. There was no resident mechanic at Back River, and I'd had to wait for an itinerant mechanic to perform the required annual inspection. He didn't come as scheduled in December, when the weather was particularly cold. Or the next two months, when – wouldn't you know it? – a strong anticyclone over Greenland blocked the warm, thawing airflow from the Gulf of Mexico.

After about three months the days warmed, the mechanic came, and I was told by telephone, "The annual inspection is now being done, and we'll repair the hole in the float as soon as we can."

"What hole?"

"We pushed the plane onto the trailer and moved it to a spot near the hangar where the mechanic could work on the plane more easily; but the plane got away from us while we were sliding her off the trailer, and the right float was punctured by the end of a two-inch pipe."

When I looked for the sheet-metal worker who had repaired the two other seaplanes based at Back River, I was told, "He's gone a-hog-huntin' in Tennessee." No-one else was able or willing to repair the hole, which was inconveniently located against the keel – hard to get at and tricky to repair, because a patch would interfere with the longitudinal strengthener that joins the two undersides of the "V"-shaped keel.

The airport cognoscenti urged that the hole, or rip, be repaired by heliarc welding. I called the manufacturer, EDO Float Company, on Long Island,

New York, and spoke to Jay Frey to confirm this, and was told that heliarcing wouldn't work for that grade of aluminum. A riveted patch was needed. As a temporary measure, I put a fiberglass patch over the hole in the float. Then, supposing that I would have to take my plane elsewhere for repairs, and fearing that the fiberglass patch wouldn't hold up to the pounding on takeoff, I placed an inflated bladder in the appropriate compartment to keep out water.

> *... a hole was broken in her bottom, which occasioned a considerable delay, as we were destitute of the materials necessary for effectual reparation.* (Mackenzie, *Voyages.*)

Who would repair the float? The seaplane bases on Long Island and at Philadelphia were closed to me because I did not have a radar transponder installed in my airplane. Nor was anyone around Baltimore willing to come out and install such a device; one radio shop suggested that I remove the wings and truck the plane to their shop! The alternatives for repairing the float were: (1) the mechanic in Kentucky, who had installed the floats, or (2) a referral from EDO: Steve Kelly's repair shop at East Haddam, CT, a little way up the Connecticut River from its mouth on Long Island Sound. Going to Kentucky would entail a 590-mile flight across the Appalachian Mountains and a problematic landing on grass at my destination. East Haddam was the obvious choice: it was in the direction of Canada, and only 365 miles away.

The first of May 1990, had come and gone. My sick airplane rested inactive on the grass outside the flight office. Beyond her little patch of shade, the sun breathed life into the pale land, seagulls followed the plow, and white sails popped out on the bay. I was eager to be on my way, but much of Canada was still frozen. I wasn't late – yet.

The direct route from Baltimore to the mouth of the Connecticut River is along the Atlantic Coast, over Philadelphia and New York City. But the air regulations decreed that I stay thirty nautical miles away from both those busy places. During the third week in May a clear spell of weather was forecast. I visited the weather bureau in person to get a thorough briefing. The day after tomorrow would be the best day, I was told. Next day I drove to Back River, anticipating an entire day to load the plane, fuel her, cut mooring lines to length, and attend to other details. Abruptly the forecast was changed. *Today* was the best day to go. But Steve Kelly didn't stay late on Thursdays. Now I was in a rush; the day was slipping away. Mike was not there – he'd moved his flying service across the bay. I asked one of the airport helpers to tow my plane down to the river. "A freebie?" he said. I was distracted. What were the new arrangements for getting to the water? With Mike's departure, they'd been changed, left to this man, who used his own tractor, and who rightly expected me to pay him. After this was settled, he pulled my plane to the water, and I took off.

Almost none of my installations worked. At the outset of the flight, at Back River, the emergency locator beacon sent out its distress signal as soon as I armed it, so I shut the thing off. The LORAN, an apparatus that looks like a taximeter and is supposed to give the plane's position over the ground – I had added it as an afterthought – wouldn't work because its portable aerial snapped. (I wasn't sorry to dump this device. It seemed inappropriate to my antique expedition.) The indications of the vertical card compass, an "improved" version of the standard magnetic compass, were badly in error; I hadn't found time to adjust the compensating magnets because of the time lost with the punctured pontoon. None of this mattered. The all-important portable transceiver radio was in working order. In the rush to get off, though, I neglected to check the mooring lines attached to the bow cleats. This would be my undoing.

Off we go! I took off from Back River, outclassed the boastful bow waves of speeding motor boats, and flew north up the bay to Havre de Grace. There I turned up the Susquehanna River, a narrow, deep river spanned at its mouth by four elegant iron bridges. After a few miles I left the Susquehanna to find the Delaware River. I maintained my direction over the ground by observing the bearing of the sun's shadow cast from tall trees along the way. (I was only five hundred feet above the ground.) Using the sun as compass, I picked up the Delaware River and followed its course some miles to the Delaware Water Gap. Near Port Jervis, New York, I left the Delaware and flew east until I came to the Hudson River, which I crossed at right angles, at West Point, NY. The visibility was more than fifty miles – I saw the trifling towers of Manhattan on the skyline – and I gloried in spending a day like this, in a way like this.

Item: Hazards of Docking

When I arrived over East Haddam, I saw a minuscule dock on the east bank of the narrow Connecticut River. I didn't like the look of it. I didn't like the wind gusting down the river. I called out my arrival over my portable radio and was acknowledged, then landed near the dock and taxied slowly toward it. There was no beach, only a dock, and docking a seaplane had been demonstrated to me once, in conditions of no wind. Now the wind had picked up and was blowing down the river so that I would have to approach the dock – upwind, into the current – on my right side. But this approach wouldn't work because I was in the left seat and the right seat was piled with gear. (*And* there was a large, uprooted tree in the water alongside the dock.)

I thought I would call on the radio and someone would walk over from the office there and help me out. But they had stopped answering the radio. I was left to myself. The wind prevented me from docking alongside, so I waited until the wind dropped, then nosed directly into the end of the dock at ninety degrees, against the wind and the current. In an instant I switched off the engine, leaped out of the cockpit and onto the float, picked up the mooring line attached to the bow cleat of the left float, and started to step ashore. But the line wasn't free – it was looped around the float's rear strut. I hadn't freed the line before leaving Back River. Just then a gust of wind stirred up little dust devils on the shore and blew the plane away from the dock, back toward a line of pilings.

Boldly I jumped into the water to save my plane, to stop it drifting away. I sank over my head and emerged, hanging helplessly onto the float spreaders, to look back under the tail, and await the collision with the pilings at the other dock. It came twenty seconds later, with a crack, as the wing tip struck a glancing blow to a piling and the water rudder was knocked off its hinges. I scrambled out of the water onto this dock. I was soaked through, mortified, and angry. Bystanders appeared. I yelled for help, and they came over and took hold of my plane. "Where are your mooring lines?" they asked. "Don't you have mooring lines?" No. Except for the bowlines, I had no mooring lines ready.

Someone lent me a dry pair of trousers, and I huffed around in these oversized jeans until I got a lift to the jet airport at New London. There I was dropped off to buy a ticket home. I waited, bedraggled, in the bar until flight time. I had a shot of whisky and looked on the good side of things: I had, after all, delivered the plane to the shop.

"I cracked up the plane," I told the strawberry blonde over the phone.
"So you won't be going, after all?"
"Oh, yes. They'll fix it in a week or so."
"Oh…"

> *Some were by no means sorry for our late misfortune, from the hope that it must put a period to our voyage, particularly as we were without a canoe.* (Mackenzie, *Voyages.*)

Came the third week in June, and the ice should have melted on the northern lakes. My plane had been repaired and was ready to be picked up.

"I'm not happy about your trip," said the strawberry blonde.
"Well, let's talk about it," I said.
"I'm jealous. You, chasing after Mackenzie . . . . .."
(*obtusely*) "Why? You're not interested in seaplaning."
"I didn't say I wanted to go."

"Well, what are you talking about, then?" I said.

"There you go. You've ended all communication. Why do you do that?"

"I can't postpone this trip," I said.

"Well, I've got some ideas of my own."

"You mean you won't be here when I get back?"

"I don't know. How long will you be gone?"

"Long enough to make the trip."

"That means you'll stay away for weeks."

[They said] *it would require several winters to get to the sea, and that old age would overtake us before the period of our return.* Mackenzie, *Voyages.*

22

COAST TO COAST IN EIGHTEEN SPLASHDOWNS

The first airplane flight across North America was by Cal Rogers in a Wright biplane in 1911, from New York City to Pasadena, flying south of the Rockies through Texas and Arizona, distance 4,231 miles. Cal was a young man in a hurry. He took ninety minutes of instruction from Wilbur Wright, bought a plane from him (christened it the Vin Fiz, after his sponsor's soft drink product, and set out to win the $50,000 Hearst Prize by crossing the continent in 30 days. He got to the coast but nineteen days too late – too many crashes and re-builds slowed him down.) My own coast-to-coast flight was 4,250 miles, coast to coast, almost identical in distance but far to the north of the route taken by the Vin Fiz. My trip, by floatplane, retraced the first crossing of North America by Alex Mackenzie in 1791-2. (It took me a lot research to find the precise route Mackenzie followed. See appendix.) Because I was frequently grounded by weather – wind on the plains, fog on the coast – my seaplane flight took all of thirty days.

<u>Day One.</u>

June 26, 1990. When I studied the Montreal chart last week I couldn't figure out the air space restrictions depicted for the city. I telephoned air traffic control and a jesting French-Canadian at the other end of the line assured me, "We don't understand them either." Before I left Back River in Baltimore I had solicited advice there. A local pilot volunteered: "Yeah, I been in Canada once, north of Montreal. I flew up to see a friend of mine who was a missionary to the Cree Indians. They lived in tipis. I helped myself to some fuel out of a fifty-five gallon drum. But I left the money."

"How long ago was that?" I asked.
"Oh, that was a long time ago."
I persisted questioning the French Canadian, and ascertained that the customs entry point nearest to Montreal that would accommodate my arrival in a floatplane was at Drummondville, Quebec, a town about sixty miles northeast of Montreal, on the St. Francis River.

From East Haddam, I flew up the Hudson, then over Lake Champlain, whose surface on this day was churned to whitecaps by the long uninterrupted fetch of the wind, and eventually I found the St Francis River. I circled over the seaplane base, got no answer to my radio call. There were two small docks. A De Havilland Beaver was at one dock, the other was vacant. After I landed, I taxied to the vacant dock, cut off the fuel and as the engine sputtered to a stop, a man caught my strut.

I saw that the second figure was a female customs agent. "I'm very happy to see you," I explained, unnecessarily. "Last time I docked without help, I fell in." She looked sympathetic and doubtful at the same time.
"How long will you be in Canada?"
"Until the end of the month."
"Where will you go in Canada?"
"To the West Coast. To British Columbia."
Again, the doubtful look. She handed me an entry permit. *Ce permis est valide jusqu'au le 30 juillet, 1990.*
"I'm going home to Texas," the strawberry blonde said, when I phoned in my position report that evening.

Day Two

The weather changed abruptly today. It turned overcast, cool, and rainy; but a good-enough day to start my quest, to retrace the first crossing of North

America. The trail started here, in Montreal, a route pioneered by French voyageurs in birch bark canoes and completed, under the leadership of Alexander Mackenzie, twenty-nine year-old partner in a fur trapping business, in 1793. Three hundred years of paddling, of finding a way by trial and error, three hundred years of wrong turns went into finding the way to the Pacific. That was then. Now I drove into Montreal in a rented car, and quite near the Lachine Rapids found Mackenzie's old fur warehouse, now a museum. The voyageurs, I learned from the guide, a good-looking blonde with a noticeable accent, trapped the beavers for their fur. To further titillate the audience, she told us that the voyageurs who transported these pelts in their canoes were so tormented with biting insects that they covered themselves with a mixture of bear grease and skunk oil to ward off the bugs. (I hoped these little darlings were low fliers.)

"What about Mackenzie? I asked.

"He left from here. From this very spot."

Day Three

The morning was overcast, gloomy. Jubilant at the prospect of the day, I went to the dock and took off from the choppy waters of the St. Francis River into a chill northwest wind. I flew up the St. Lawrence until I came to the white water of the Lachine Rapids and the old fur warehouse that I visited yesterday. I was on Mackenzie's trail and I intended to stay on it. By the time I came to the end of Montreal Island, the overcast had cleared, replaced by cloud streets of cumulus. Here I picked up the fork of the Ottawa River, which I would follow for three hundred miles, to its tributary, the Mattawa, and its source at Trout Lake. One single image dominated today's flight: the Ottawa River flowing from the western horizon, the first of the glorious waterways I expected to follow, speeding joyfully to the west.

When I came to the fork where the Ottawa curves off northwest, I followed the pretty little Mattawa River to Lake Nipissing. This is a big lake, about forty miles long. My intended landing area was just short of it, on the smaller Trout Lake (itself directly on the Voyageurs' Highway). Seaplanes are constrained to fly from one sheltered lake to another, not to brave large open areas of water like Lake Nipissing. (By the way, Trout Lake is where a crew from Hollywood made the 1942 film "Captains of the Clouds.")

Day Four

Grounded at Trout Lake by weather fronts over Manitoba and Ontario. I was dependent for transportation on taxis from North Bay chauffeured by garrulous drivers who made their business mine – modern-day voyageurs all too ready to tell of their arduous lives. "I was stressed! I was worn to a frazzle!" the first taxi driver recounted. "I was incontinent! I went to the doctor. 'I can't find nothing,' the doc told me. 'What is your work schedule? Ah ha!' he said. 'There's your problem.'" A second taxi driver, desperately navigating a maze of back streets, told me, "We're desperate for more traffic lights! Desperate!"
"All we got here," a third driver complained, "is snow and ice through April. Rain ever since. I'm depressed. I can't stand it."

[The voyageurs] go in canoes, laden with packs of fur, which, from the immense length of the voyage …is a most severe trial of patience and perseverance…and proceed in great measure day and night… a life of unremitting exertion, till their strength is lost in premature old age. (Mackenzie)

Day Five

Another rainy day in North Bay. I walked into town and came to a sign, "RAW FUR BUYER." "How is your business?" I asked. "Bad. There's no demand. It's the animal-rights activists."

Day Six

The sky this morning was marvelously clear, all the way to the western horizon. A fresh wind carried the sharp smell of pine needles across Trout Lake. After several days of cloud and rain, I could believe that this bright new day was the first day of creation, or at the very least, a new-minted silver dollar. Once in the air, I reached for my chart – the one I had marked with the course – but couldn't find it, and I circled Trout Lake, guessing it had slipped under the my seat during take-off. I searched the cockpit and found a one-million scale chart I could use. Christ! A radio transmitter tower loomed just ahead at my level. Instantly, I banked away from the tower. Then I flew straight and level to get over my scare.

The distance from Trout Lake to Thunder Bay, on the shore of Lake Superior, is 610 air miles, mostly along the shores of lakes Huron and Superior. About half way along this route there is a convenient alighting point, at Wa Wa Lake, just inland from the northeast corner of Lake Superior and the old fur-trading post of Michipicoten. From Trout Lake I headed west over Lake Nipissing and found the French River. "Scenic rapids," I scribbled, and followed the French downstream to its mouth on Georgian Bay. "Azure. Emerald in the shoals. Purple cloud shadows," I noted. Today the weather was superb. But yesterday, while I was on the ground, poking around North Bay, waiting out the bad weather, a small plane crashed here in Georgian Bay, killing its three occupants.

I arrived over Sault Ste. Marie at 12.30P, and turned north up the eastern shore of Superior. Fog lay all along Superior's shore, and I followed a power line that parallels the coast a few miles inland. (This is the rim of the Canadian Shield – no place for a forced landing.) After an hour's flying, zipping over the trees, I saw Wa Wa Lake, clear of fog. There below me was a dock with a seaplane. I landed nearby and taxied up to it, but no-one came. There was no wind, so I cut the engine and got on the left float, and paddled my plane, like a canoe, gently to the dock. I hopped on to the dock, caught the strut, and tied my float to a dockside cleat – my first successful unaided docking. I walked to the shack on the dock, but it was locked, though not deserted, for a watchdog was tied outside.

After a while, someone drove up and fetched the owner, and my plane was refueled. I taxied out to takeoff "the short way", straight across that little lake, and directly into the wind. (I don't have much practice at crosswind takeoffs in a seaplane.) I opened the throttle to force the little airplane onto the "step" under the floats. The shore was coming up fast. I pulled back on the yoke, and – damn! – the heels of the floats stuck in the water and slowed the airplane down. I pushed the yoke forward to pick up speed again. The shore was much nearer when the airplane unstuck from the water. I glanced at the air speed indicator. It flickered between forty and fifty mph. ("I got the wrong prop on this plane," I mouthed.) Large in the windshield were the houses on the shore and the telephone poles and a garage with a red roof. I skimmed over the garage with the red roof as my propeller clawed us into the sky. (Take heed, novice seaplaners, of my blunders.)

Soon came the big grain elevators of Thunder Bay. The seaplane landing area is within a breakwater at the north end of this harbor. I snatched another look at the *Water Aerodrome Supplement*, which I had handy in the cockpit. Under *Remarks*, it noted "Heavy swells. Exposed to S & E winds with heavy seas." But right now, a light south wind was blowing, so I expected no problem. I banked over the seaplane dock. The air was unaccountably bumpy. The inclinometer ball skidded to the right. I pushed the right rudder pedal to center the ball and straighten the airplane, then approached low over the shore on a south heading, lined up into the wind and, I noticed (uncomprehending) with the entrance to the breakwater, exposing myself to the swells. BOUNCE. BOUNCE. My airplane pitched like a see-saw in the swell; when I tried to turn back to the shore, she rolled alarmingly and the wing tips alternately dipped very near the water. I yelled an impolite version of "I hate seaplanes." (I would have been doubly scared had I known that the water temperature was 36F!)

I tried to drift backwards ("sail") to the dock. With the propeller still turning, I made no progress towards the dock, though the little seaplane pitched like a rocking horse in the swell. This swell, I suddenly realized, was from *yesterday's* wind. A lamentable principle intruded upon my mind: "The most stable position for a floatplane on the water is *upside down.*" I turned the seaplane broadside to the swells, gingerly working rudder and ailerons, and got her facing downwind, away from the harbor entrance. The seaplane bucketed along toward the dock. There was no-one there, and I knew I couldn't dock the seaplane myself. But here, too, I had telephoned ahead. When I neared the shore, a man came out of a shack and motioned me to a ramp. (Thank God for Alexander Graham Bell.) I drove the airplane up the ramp and cut the engine. I got out of the plane.

"You don't mind taking on Lake Superior, do you!" the man said.

"That was as much swell as I want to handle," I said.

"It was as much swell as anyone would want to handle. You should have landed close against the breakwater, away from the entrance."

There is a hydraulic lift here to move a floatplane from the dock ramp to a parking space on shore, but the narrow spread of my floats didn't fit this lift. As we struggled to pull the floatplane up the ramp, my leg went through a hole in the rotted planking and came out bruised and bloodied.

I had had more thrills than I cared for in one day: the scare with the radio transmitter tower at Trout Lake, the botched takeoff at Wa Wa, the landing in heavy swell at Thunder Bay. I pumped out the floats and took a taxi to town, where I checked into this hotel, near the waterfront.

"You want a coffee?"

"No. Give me a whisky."

(Doubtful) "You want CC "(Canadian Club Whisky)?

(Goes away; returns; still doubtful.) "You want CC then?"

"Yes. Do you have soda?"

(Relieved) "You want a Coke, eh?"

"Just bring the whisky."

I drank the CC and contemplated "seconds."

"Here's your coffee."

Author's note: I can't explain the seeming reluctance to serve liquor, but Mackenzie himself noted that "it is a practice throughout the North-West neither to sell or give any rum...during the summer."

The voyageurs were whisky enthusiasts though, and no doubt would have appreciated the girl in the kitchen, too. What is the dirty apron, the soiled T-shirt, the hair tumbled over her face, to the arresting figure of the splendidly nubile siren in the scullery, toiling over the pots and pans?

Day Seven

Thunder Bay, July 2, 1990. To this *entrepot* at Fort William the voyageurs averaged eight weeks from Lachine, paddling up to eighteen hours a day. It had taken me fifteen flying hours. And I am behind schedule already. But I am bound to take a day off to visit Old Fort William. Besides, I postpone for a while the unknown hazards of my trip. The voyageurs, as many as twelve hundred of them, according to Mackenzie, spent much of July here. In between carrying ninety-pound packages of fur, two or three at a time, over the portage, they rested, "indulging themselves in the free use of liquor."

Day Eight

Thunder Bay, July 3. The weather turned bad today. I went to the seaplane base and pumped out the floats, then walked around town. In the Grain Bin Bar sat a circle of old-timers, lively with liquor.
"I worked for the CP railroad," someone announced.
"No! When?"
"1945 to 1958."
"Stop! You knew Joe Sigaleri!"
"No, I didn't."
"Everyone knew him!"
"I didn't know him," said a third man.

"He was the best dynamite man in Canada! Before he went back to Italy, he went and smashed that big piano of his. He took an axe and did it. I could have killed him. It was worth ninety dollars to me."

<u>Day Nine</u>

Thunder Bay, July 4, 1990. The weather cleared on this third day. The lines were loosened from the float cleats and I was pushed off from the dock. Then the engine failed to start. So much for the new battery installed at the beginning of my trip. My helpers had not released their hold on the tail, or the seaplane would have drifted back and fouled the adjoining dock, whose sides were too high to clear the tail plane. (It is possible to "prop" the engine by hand, but this is of no use if, as happened to me now, the pilot must start the engine at a moment's notice. Seven loons – I counted them – floated nearby, laughing.

The mechanic diagnosed a bad solenoid, so I rode with him into town in a ponderous old Pontiac to search the auto parts stores for a replacement. When the new part was installed, around 2.00P, I telephoned the weatherman. The route to Kenora, he said, was VFR (that is to say, clear of low clouds). "What's the surface wind forecast?" I remembered to ask.
"Wind gusting to twenty-five knots."
"I'm not going," I said.

The thought occurs to me that my timetable doesn't make enough allowance for the wind.

<u>Day Ten</u>

Thunder Bay, July 5, 1990. The morning dawned bright in Thunder Bay, though fog was expected at Fort Francis until 11.00A. I went to the harbor, sniffed the cool air, and put on my life jacket. Today the wind blew offshore (opposite to the wind's direction of four days ago). I taxied out to the breakwater, turned into wind, and took off to the northeast, committing myself once more to the disorganized domains of sky and bush. Once in the air, I oriented myself with the shore, then flew west along the railroad, under a layer of stratocumulus clouds, and over a two-tone forest of dark conifers and pale broadleaves. A big hole in the overcast over Rainy Lake let the sun shine though to change the lake's color from gray to blue. From Rainy Lake, which is very irregularly shaped, I came to Rainy River, a placid river flowing through fertile farmlands.

Following Rainy River, I came to Lake of the Woods, a very conspicuous feature on the chart. (It is about sixty miles long and the same wide, with a reputed 14,600 islands and 25,000 miles of shoreline.) At its north end the chart shows Kenora, site of the portage to the Winnipeg River. Keeping my finger on the chart, I followed the shoreline north. The irregular shapes of the land and water coastlines defeated my efforts. There was no sign of Kenora where it should have been. Just clouds, trees and water. A vague unease settled on me. Twenty minutes later I saw a town and concluded it might be Kenora – way off to the right, where it wasn't supposed to be. There was no sun and the sky had completely clouded over.

The voyageurs seem to have got lost more often in Lake of the Woods than in all the other miles of their long voyage put together. (Morse, *Fur Trade Canoe Routes*).

I landed at Kenora – there was even a man to help me tie up. Once out of the airplane, I walked across the road with my bags, checked into this hotel, and sat down to lunch. "I shoot thirty or forty dogs a year round my place," announced a diner at the next table. "Keeps 'em away from the chickens."

Day Eleven

July 6, 1990. A clear blue sky here in Kenora. Forecast for The Pas: "Scattered clouds at five thousand feet, light rain showers, surface wind 190 degrees at seven knots." "What's the best refueling stop?" I inquired of he dispatcher. "Better stop at Riverton, on the far shore of Lake Winnipeg," he said.

From Lake of the Woods the Winnipeg River winds through a wilderness of lakes on the southern edge of the Canadian Shield, then flows west across the prairies. (Six great dams have all but eliminated the many rapids and falls of Mackenzie's day.) The brightness had faded from the western sky. Over Lake Winnipeg the sky was leaden and the brown water was whipped to whitecaps by a south wind – the counter-clockwise air flow around an approaching low-pressure system.

This (Lake Winnipeg) can only be the Japan Sea. (French explorer, about 1670.)

I flew directly across Lake Winnipeg, due west, then turned north along its shore to Riverton, where the narrow Icelandic River empties into the lake. The river looked pretty small, and I toyed with the idea of overflying this gas stop (not a realistic option) and going on to The Pas. But the western horizon was now dark, belying the original forecast, so I decided to land. I circled the dock twice. There was no sign of life, and I buzzed the town a couple of times, then landed on the river. Despite is tiny size, Riverton is a major seaplane base with a dock full of floatplanes. As yet there was no answer on the radio, and I taxied in circles on the little river until a man appeared at the dock and made room for me by untying one of the float-planes and moving it forward one space. My helper was the pilot of a de Havilland Otter based here. An hour after I had tied up, it started to rain.

Later, I accompanied the Otter pilot and his pals on a tour of the town. The first of three watering holes was the licensed beverage room annexed to my hotel. I answered their queries the best I could. One of the party, unsteady on his feet, announced that I was lost. It was the only explanation for some-one to be flying around by himself, apparently aimlessly, and asking all sorts of questions.

"Maybe he's looking for something?" said a wit.

(As always, my mention of Mackenzie was met by a blank stare.)

"Maybe he's looking for stories?" persisted another.

The Otter pilot perked up. "A month sitting on the dock at Little Grand Rapids will give anyone a year of stories," he said.

"About what?" I asked.

"Indians," he said.

Day Twelve

Saturday, July 7, 1990. Still at Riverton, grounded by bad weather. There was a carnival in town, with half a dozen rides, some side shows, and a nail-pounding contest. A man had bought his four dogs to town and tied them to his pick-up "to get them used to people."

Day Thirteen

Sunday July 8, 1990. Sky clear. Forecast for my route to The Pas: "altocu-mulus castellanus and isolated towering cumulonimbus." After takeoff from Riverton, I checked out my two compasses by flying the section lines of this bit of farmed countryside. Errors averaged twenty-nine degrees for the verti-cal compass and a mere seventeen degrees for the alcohol compass.

The town of The Pas is on the banks of the Saskatchewan River, but the seaplane base is situated at the more suitable Grace Lake, a half mile south of the river and three miles east of town. When I arrived over Grace Lake at 1.00P, rain showers lay to the west of the town, and a stiff breeze sent parallel white wind lines across the lake. I had called the operator a couple of days before. "Go to the dock beside the house," he said.

I saw two seaplane docks from the air – but no sign of people. I landed dead into the wind and taxied to the dock beside the house. No-one was there. No answer on the radio, either. I couldn't dock the plane myself, because the wind was blowing off the dock, which – to complicate matters – was too tall to clear my tailplane. I taxied to the second dock. It seemed deserted, but I saw a man in a red jacket. I got his attention and pointed to the dock, indicating that I wanted to tie up. It wasn't at all obvious to me where I should go, and he guided me by hand signals into a shallow basin, covered with algae.

The wind made steering difficult. My airplane would in no wise taxi across the wind: she wanted to *weathercock* into the wind. I tried to beach the plane on a mud bank, but cut the power too soon, and she drifted back, downwind. I threw a line ashore, twice, to the man in red. Both times it fell short. There was a lull in the wind. With the cockpit door open to catch what wind there was, I tried to "sail" the plane backwards, to the far side of the little basin where I saw there was space to beach an airplane. The wind fell calm. I got out onto the float and paddled the airplane backwards. Just then the wind sprang up and the rain pelted down. The floatplane picked up speed and drifted toward a docked Cessna 185. "Start her up!" yelled Red Jacket. I jumped into the cockpit and turned the ignition key. Nothing! Damn that solenoid!

The wind kept pushing my seaplane toward the other floatplanes. I tried to guide her with the air rudder. I shouted to Red Jacket to get on the 185 float and fend off my plane from impending disaster. He sprinted along the dock and scrambled on to the right front float of the 185 just in time to fend off my plane, while I danced ineffectually on my plane's left float. The left wing of my plane passed under the right wing of the bigger 185.

When he had secured my plane to the dock, Red Jacket introduced himself. His name was Bruce Pelechaty, chief fire warden in this district.

"I would have jumped in if it would have helped," he said cheerfully.

"How deep is it?" I asked.

"Not very deep, but there's two feet of loon s— [mud] on the bottom."

Day Fourteen

Still grounded until the starter is fixed. My seaplane lies at the dock, checked occasionally by curious muskrats.

<u>Day Fifteen</u>

About half of the population here in The Pas is Indian. "All of them speak the Indian language," I was told. "Mostly Cree." Later, when I switched on the radio, I listened to a Cree radio program. It sounded guttural – like Chinese. (So, the Orient must be near, as the early explorers had believed!) Then I read, in a "Guide to The Pas", of a radio program that had been started by one Murray Mackenzie. Where could I find him? I decided to visit the Swampy Crees. The name has a gloomy, water-logged ring to it, but is the only tribe listed in the directory that is explicitly Cree, the same tribe as Murray Mackenzie, of radio fame. I went on to the street, hailed a taxi, and gave the driver the address. "That's the shopping mall you want," he said. "All Indian-owned." The driver was an Indian (or a Metis? I couldn't tell.) "Do you work for the circus?" he asked. Evidently, news of my antics in Ontario and Manitoba had preceded me? And what else could I be <u>but</u> the advance man for the circus that had come to town? It was my Sears work shirt that identified me, a stranger, as a manual worker most likely connected to the circus. (I didn't find Murray, but got into some entertaining misunderstandings in my search.)

That evening, I telephoned Carolyn.
"Where were you when you called the other night?" she asked.
"Lake Winnipeg."
"Do you realize that you didn't talk any sense? And that was my mother you spoke to? I had already gone to bed…"

<u>Day Sixteen</u>

July 11, 1990. As soon as Roy Boyes had fixed my airplane's generator (for that was the cause of the starting problem that had bedeviled me since Baltimore), I was ready to leave. At eleven o'clock I started my takeoff run on the glassy water of Grace Lake. Once off the water I climbed all the way to eight hundred feet and followed the Saskatchewan River west as it meanders through the poorly-drained green muskeg and algae-covered lakes and ponds.

At Amisk Lake, I was over the Canadian Shield again, the land of clouds, trees and water. The canoe trail follows the Sturgeon-Weir through the shield to the Frog Portage and over to the Churchill River which flows for a thousand miles to Hudson Bay. (Easier said than done: the Churchill is more a series of connected lakes than a river – and these amidst a great wilderness of other, unconnected lakes. In other words, I couldn't make head or tail of the chart: the Churchill is well nigh indistinguishable from the air, entwined as it is by a hundred thousand lakes. How would I find Frog Portage?

I followed a rare highway (Route 106) to the west, couldn't find the Frog Portage, and steered in the direction I hoped would bring me to Lac La Ronge. When I found that large lake, I looked for the seaplane base that the chart showed at its west end. I circled once and approached over the town into a southeast wind. There was an immediate answer to my radio call, and I was direcred to the Air Sask ramp. I landed and taxied over to this ramp, and was guided to a mooring by one of their pilots, who rode on my right float and picked up the line from a buoy. There we waited for a tender to take us back to the dock. Within a half-hour I was on a balcony of a dock-side hotel overlooking my floatplane, with a view of the other side of the lake, twenty miles away. The temperature was perfect, the day refreshing, with the pleasant sound of the waves lapping against the shore.

Day Seventeen

Last night my plane jumped her buoy, which was now between the floats. But the wind was not gusty enough to capsize the little seaplane. Providence. This morning I left Lac La Ronge and set out for Lake Athabaska, with a refueling stop planned at Buffalo Narrows. I flew up the Churchill River, about twenty-five miles north, but failed almost immediately to follow its zigzag progress through the puzzling pattern of lakes. I picked up my bearings at the tiny town of Pinehouse Lake, from the sun reflected from its asbestos roofs and gravel roads. Forty miles further up the Churchill (easy to follow now, away from the Shield), I came to Buffalo Narrows. Here I landed and tied up – with help – so that my tailplane projected safely beyond the end of the rickety dock. After I refueled the plane, I telephoned the weatherman for the route forecast to Fort Chipewyan. "There's a line of thunderstorms near Fort McMurray. It'll probably clear by four o'clock," he said. "They're always forecasting thunderstorms that don't appear" grumbled the dispatcher.

At 4:00P I called the weatherman again (he was two hundred miles south, in North Battleford). He opined it would be "OK to go." The sky was clear, he said, except for isolated, towering cumulus. But I took another look at the white caps on the lake here and decided that the wind was too strong to takeoff from Buffalo Narrows. (I remembered Mike Forster: "If there are white caps on the water, there's too much wind for a small sea-plane.") The dispatcher, unsympathetic, said, "You'll probably have to sell your plane here."

The wind picked up force and banged my floatplane against the dock, from which it was protected only by a couple of small flotation cushions I had with me. I walked down the road to a garage, cadged two bald tires, and hung them over the dock as bumpers, one at each end of the near float. An osprey hovered overhead, facing into wind, hunting for fish.

After securing the airplane, I checked into the motel that is situated on the little isthmus between Peter Pond Lake and Churchill Lake.
"This us Churchill Lake, then?" I said, by way of greeting, to the desk clerk.
"Don't know," he answered.
"Been here long?"
"Eleven years." He smiled complacently.

Day Eighteen

Buffalo Narrows. Friday, July 13, 1990. Grounded. A hot, windy day, eighty-six degrees Fahrenheit, whitecaps on the water. After breakfast I walked up and down the town's few streets, then, for want of anything else to do, ended up back at the café, where there was always conversation to while away the time. This morning, a dolorous Frenchman was telling the sad but entertaining history of his boisterous life with a Cree Indian woman with a predilection, when she was liquored up, of kicking out windows, or, more emphatically, throwing a washtub through one.

Day Nineteen

Buffalo Narrows. Saturday, July 14, 1990. The wind still blew. Main Street was deserted except for a solitary raven hopping along the center of the road. Later in the morning, the wind veered to the northwest and picked up strength, gusting to twenty-eight knots. My floatplane was now tail-on to the wind. Heavy gusts pushed down on the spring-loaded flaps from behind, causing them to bang up and down. The airplane jerked around on its lines, fighting the powerful urge to weathercock into the wind. I was hesitant about turning the airplane to face the wind, but one of the seaplaners said, "It's OK. You can hold her on a line like a pet dog on a leash." He turned my airplane into the wind, where she lay quiet against the dock facing the opposite direction, with the flaps not banging anymore, mercifully quiet.

Showers and low clouds were expected all day. Nothing for it but to go back to the café.

"Pemmican, you say? Never heard of it. Now, moose meat…I shot a moose a few years back, and gave it to my wife to cut into strips and dry over a fire while I went fishing. Next thing I knew, she'd burned down the whole island!"

"La Loche? Don't go there. They'll steal your plane and anything else you've got by the end of the day. It's that kind of town. Not like this place, Buffalo Narrows – you won't find a more respectable town in the north than this."

The trapper finished, the door of the café swung open, and in strode a constable of the RCMP, manly in bearing, smart in his pressed uniform with polished leather pistol holster. Silence fell. The Indians and the drunks and the rest of us stared at the constable like schoolboys eying their headmaster. The constable went up to the unshaven cook, who, elbows on the counter, was dragging on a cigarette. "Come with me," said the constable in a low voice, jerking his head toward the door. They went outside and, through the window, we could see the constable lecturing the crestfallen took.

"What did he want? You in trouble?" someone asked.

"He said the egg-and-bacon sandwich he took out of here this morning crumbled all over the front of his uniform, and he had to go back to the barracks and change, and it better not happen again."

Day Twenty

Another overcast morning and the northwest wind did not diminish, and my floatplane was still pinned to the water. So even though I should be on my way *back* from the Pacific Coast by now, I returned to the café. An Indian came in, sat next to me, introduced himself as Mcdonald.

"I'm a Chip. [Chipewyan] I got two wives and nine children."

"Is it a secret?"

"No. They're all right here in town."

"They're not jealous of each other?"

"No. They both treat me very well. Hey, I'm supporting fifteen children and my first wife that left me six years ago. Here comes one of them now."

One of the wives approached McD, without apparent enthusiasm, and shook hands with him. She had a stocky build and wore a sweatshirt proclaiming "Couch Potato."

Day Twenty-One

OK to go! After a bone-shaking take-off from Lake Churchill, I headed for Fort Chipewyan. I see from my log book that I flew for 3.7 hours via Lac La Loche, the Clearwater River, and the Athabaska River – three hundred miles in all. The Athabaska is a wide, muddy river flowing through a hundred thousand square miles of wilderness. Lowering clouds now covered all the sky, and it was comforting to fly along the big river, knowing that I could not get lost. Still, I opened the throttle to get to Fort Chipewyan as soon as I could. There was little traffic on the river – a barge, the odd seaplane – and only the occasional tiny settlement on its banks. By the time I got to Fort Chip, rain showers blotted out the western end of Lake Athabaska, and instead of flying direct I approached the town from the east. This is a huge lake, and I planned to alight on the more sheltered Small Lake just northeast of town There I set my plane down on the water, and taxied in, gratified to see a man come out to meet me.

"Are you Mark?"

"Yes."

"I talked to you on the phone."

"Yes. We've had lousy weather for the last two days. Rain, and thirty-knot winds."

Mark drove me to this hotel, The Lodge, which is on a granite outcrop overlooking Lake Athabaska, a yellow sea under a dismal sky. (The hotel is almost empty of guests.)

"About the only thing worth seeing in Fort Chip is the Chinese waitress at the Athabaska Café," said Mark.

Day Twenty-Two

July 17, 1990. A dismal day, rainy and cold. Mackenze was based here eight years. Even today, Fort Chip is not connected to anywhere by road, except by snow road in winter, yet it is a completely urban environment, with automobiles, telephones, videos, a laundromat…Despite the superabundance of water, none is available to drink today, and the restaurants, two or three in number, are closed because the town water supply has become polluted with industrial pollutants from Fort McMurray. Anyway, the restaurants are closed, and the glory of the town, the Chinese waitress must remain a traveler's tale.

8.00 P. A light gray sky over the metallic lake. The bad weather may be moving out. Maybe I can fly out of here tomorrow?

Day Twenty-Three

Still grounded. Mackenzie reported that "of all the Indian nations, the Cree women are the most comely."

"Oh, yes!" agreed a pilot. "Some of the Cree girls <u>are</u> good-looking. I'm working on one right now. It's slow. I'm taking her up tomorrow for a flying lesson."

Day Twenty-Four

July 19, 1990. Still at Fort Chip. What a letdown! I woke to find the sky gray, the low clouds still scudding overhead. I wasn't going anywhere until the weather was good and ready. I foresaw an inconsequential day ahead of me, a walk to the coin laundry in the rain. By 9.00A, though, the forecast made good and the sky cleared rapidly from the west. I hurriedly packed my things to leave. I'd fly west as far as I could down the Peace (three hours it turned out to be, before the clouds built up) along a broad avenue in the sky, between banks of clouds on the north and south horizons.

Of some settlements marked on the chart, there was no sign. (Place names marked on Canadian maps tend to be optimistic: the only remaining evidence of one place, still marked, is said to be an old bath tub. I did see, though, a hamlet of five cabins next to a wide water fall (Vermilion Falls). The forecast is for thundery conditions today but drier air tomorrow, so I'm staying here tonight, at the town of High Level, Alberta.

Day Twenty-Five

I flew into the Rocky Mountains today, in two legs: to Charlie Lake (Fort St. John, BC) and on to Prince George, BC. My air time was 7.1 hours. The entrance to the Rockies is at the gorge where they've dammed the mighty Peace River. Above this dam, at Lake Williston, steep snow-capped mountains rise to six or seven thousand feet, dwarfing my little Cessna, whose wings were rocked by air currents as I flew her through the gorge.

Here I made a mistake in re-tracing Mackenzie's track. At the junction of the Pack and Parsnip Rivers, I took the more inviting valley of the Pack River. Mackenzie had taken the Parsnip River, which took him farther East than he needed to go, and resulted in the smash-up of his canoe.

When I called Carolyn this evening, she said, "I don't know how you think you're going to make it to Manhattan by the end of the month."
"Oh, we'll figure something out," I said.
"What's this 'we,' white man?" she said, playing the part of Tonto to the Lone Ranger.

Day Twenty-Six

July 21, 1990. Tabor Lake, Prince George. A clear night with bright stars slowly gave way to the dawn. A coyote howled from the opposite hill. Morning came, clear, and the water very still. The surface of the lake was like glass and I thought I should wait for some wind. When it didn't come, I untied the mooring lines and silently paddled the over-loaded floatplane away from the shore. Then I climbed into the cockpit and started the engine, though reluctant to demolish the silence of the morning.

From Lake Tabor, I flew fifty miles down the fast-flowing Fraser until I came to Mackenzie's West Road River, which descends 135 miles from the forested plateau. I was flying over a wilderness inaccessible except on foot or by seaplane. The route Mackenzie "discovered" was an Indian "grease trail," a trade route for taking the congealed oil of the candle fish inland. Because of its difficulty, the route is impracticable for modern commerce, and no paved road or railroad follows it today. Mackenzie's route then enters the foothills of the Coast Mountains. Mackenzie's party supposedly went around the east flank of what is now called Mount Mackenzie. But the aeronautical chart seems to represent, in tinted contours, a pass aligned north-south on the west flank of Mount Mackenzie, butted against the Bella Coola Valley. This pass, I thought, would be the best route for a low-flying airplane.

I was now flying south at five hundred feet above the ground – five thousand feet above sea level – and could not see the pass that I had noted on the half-million chart. I made a climbing 360 degree turn to gain another two thousand feet altitude, and re-oriented myself with Tanya Lakes, back there over my left shoulder. My objective, the Bella Coola River valley, remained hidden, just as it had to Mackenzie.

Once in the valley of the Bella Coola, flying west in the still air, below the level of the surrounding peaks, with the Pacific Ocean now visible, I relaxed, and speculated on the distance to China. Below me was a small airport, supposedly equipped with a "remote communications outlet." I called out my position. To my surprise, I was instantly answered by a cheerful voice, distant I don't know how many capes and promontories. "Do you still plan on Bella Bella?" "Yes," I answered.

I passed over the little town of Bella Coola and along the pale turquoise fiord called North Bentinck Arm, which is walled in by snow-capped mountains. I had merely to find my way through the fiords to Dean Channel, to take the third turn to the left, as shown on the chart to reach my destination. But by now I realized that I was on the wrong side of King Island. I was flying about three thousand feet lower than the mountain peaks on either side of me and I climbed to fly through a high pass across King Island (so named by George Vancouver, who had mapped the area only seven weeks before Mackenzie arrived in these waters).

The route had looked obvious enough when I was sitting in the hotel last night, looking at the chart. But the real world of flying in the mountains is not the flatness of a chart but a place of vertical perspectives. Eventually I saw a place that could only be Bella Bella, shining in the sun. I picked out a landing path to avoid floating logs strewn about the harbor, and alighted on the Pacific Ocean.

"Where you from?"

"Montreal."

"Hey! This guy came all the way from Montreal! In a little plane like that!"

Day Twenty-Seven

Fog lingered all day. "We're supposed to be in New York next week," said Carolyn on the phone. "Why don't you just leave the plane where you are? I'm afraid you'll kill yourself otherwise." (OK. I'd park the airplane on the west coast and jet back east.)

Day Twenty-Eight

More Fog. I decided to park my seaplane near Seattle, and headed south, and was in the air 2.1 hours before turning back to land at my starting point, Shearwater. (I turned back at the top of Queen Charlotte Sound because of fog.) "I'm going to try to get to Vancouver overland," I told Carl, the fish-spotter pilot.

"Don't do it," said Carl. "I've known too many who didn't make it through those passes."

Day Twenty-Nine

I took Carl's advice – went by sea. I had to wait until 4.00P; then flew under low stratus via Egg Island lighthouse, Alert Bay, and Discovery Passage to land at Campbell River, B.C. after 2.5 hours flight time.

Day Thirty

I flew to Friday Harbor (State of Washington), and thence to Bellingham (Float Haven) where I parked the seaplane. Total flight time, 2.2 hours.

<u>Day Thirty-One</u>

I rode a jetliner from Seattle back East, to Washington D.C. The flight across the continent took 4 hours and twenty-eight minutes. (Float Haven would find a buyer for my airplane. I had to get on with my life.)

[This is a condensed account of my book *Tracking Mackenzie to the Sea*, 1990.]

23

FLYING TO CHINA

My coast-to-coast floatplane trip left me with a vast, unsatisfied curiosity about China. What was so special about this perennial quest object over the western horizon that caused the explorers to cross the Atlantic, then canoe across North America east to west to reach it? "Simple," you say. "That old promoter Marco Polo conned them into it."

Five years after my seaplane flight to the Pacific, I got what I'd been angling for, a telephone call from Hyper Bank asking me to undertake a trip to China (I had been working my contacts). Finally I would go – would check out China, goal of Columbus, the French explorer-canoeists, and the pontooning Lindberghs.

Tuesday, 10/3/1995. I set off for the East by flying west. (My itinerary: Washington to San Francisco, five-and-one-half hours; S.F. to Tokyo, ten and one-half hours; Tokyo to Beijing, five hours.) I boarded the airplane at Dulles with my hand baggage and squeezed down the aisle of the plane. My many attempts to cram these bags onto the overhead provoked a fitful rain of pillows and folded blankets, which fell onto a Japanese business man, already seated. He smiled at first, then turned thoughtful as more pillows came down. I arrived at Beijing in the dark (in every way). But the airport officials were young, smart, and helpful; and all printed signs – nice surprise – were in Chinese *and* English. In no time I was outside. Jubilant, I hailed a taxi at the curb. "Xin Da Du Hotel!" I told the driver. A broad grin was the response. (The natives were friendly!)

Next day, early, I went up to breakfast in the dining room. It was almost empty at this hour. The head waiter asked for my room number. "Six-O-One," I said. The three waitresses standing against the wall pricked up their ears, stared at me intently, then looked at each other. "Six Oh Won, Sex Oh Won," they mimicked. (But shyly.) These girls, a fresh draft from the countryside no doubt, were evidently surprised, intrigued, delighted. "Six Oh Won." Can monkeys talk? Well, this alien could! (It was later explained to me. The enormity of China, its 5,000 year culture and long isolation make the Chinese naturally self-referencing.)

After breakfast I went into the street and encountered hordes of Han people, crowds of orderly, serene Chinese, walking and cycling, their eyeglasses styled just like mine, the ones I paid too much for in Washington, D.C. In the nearby park, I came upon a group of middle-aged couples waltzing to music in three-quarter time among groves of very old cypress trees – gnarled, furrowed, and warty. Another group encircled one of these venerable trees, an arbor vitae, while meditating to the soothing music of a cassette player. (The arbor vitae tree is called canoewood in Canada. It cured Jacques Cartier's men of scurvy, when they were searching for China along the St Lawrence River.) Two persons passed me, side-by-side, chatting, walking backwards. There were no strained expressions on any of the faces I saw. (This was not the world I knew.) A man stood in front of a very old tree shored up by poles. He was alternately bowing to the tree, then shouting an acclamation. Over there, a group of fifty persons sang, full-throated, in a pavilion among the trees. A solitary man walking along the path toward me unexpectedly gave tongue: do re mi fa sol la ti do!

Here in Beijing I joined up briefly with other members of our numerous team before it was split into small teams and dispatched to the outer reaches of the empire "to correctly finance the commercialization of the state farm lands." I was assigned to Team No. 6. "You will go first to Kunming, where you will be warmly welcomed." (One team was sent to the Himalayas and would freeze the entire time; others to the great valleys of the Yellow River and the Yangtse and elsewhere. I had the best assignment, I was told. Xishuangbanna, pronounced Shishwanbanah (the name means "twelve districts of one thousand mu of paddy fields each"), is China's Florida. "It is feeling perching oasis," I was assured.

Our team consisted of two extraverted Frenchmen, one introverted Englishman with a photo of a pet rabbit in his wallet, myself (chief scribe), and four Chinese (two soft-spoken women, two impassive males). My French vocabulary was limited ("A bas les vins etrangeres!"), and my Chinese vocab ended at "Knee How!" for Hello! Luckily the two Frenchmen spoke English. There appeared to be no hope of learning Chinese. If English words were deconstructed into syllables and put into a cement mixer, regurgitated, and uttered by someone with a stone in his mouth (the resulting noise punctuated with little grunts), then you would have Chinese. Surprisingly, there are points where English and Chinese converge and briefly overlap. I was told that by a happy chance "Pepsi Cola" means "Everything is very happy!" and Coca Cola means "I am happy while I eat!"

Kunming, a place the size of Kansas City, is at six thousand feet elevation. (Marco Polo described it as a large and splendid city – but did he go there?) Upon arrival, we were assigned two interpreters. No. 1 Frenchman immediately named the leader "Illary" ("Shillary" in Chinese) because of her bossy manner – a reference to the then First Lady of the United States. Illary explained, "I study Oxford Dictionary for six months with object to learn ten thousand useful words. This way I reach peak of perfection." Did the second interpreter proceed similarly? We don't know. She was too shy to say anything. She only said "Oh." She had two ways of saying this: "Oh!" (surprised), and "Oh?" (puzzled). We called her Miss Oh. First item on the agenda was an official luncheon. Entering the restaurant, we passed cages of live animals, reptiles and fowls. There was a cage of writhing snakes and an angry lizard, larger than a cat. We were directed to sit at a large round table, at the center of which was a lazy Susan with a dozen dishes piled with food. Chicken feet, eel, peanuts, bean curd, pig livers, bamboo shoots, spiny crab, and frogs were on offer. No. 1 Frenchman said, "Don't assume that the Chinese eat all these strange things because they are hungry. No. They are adventurous omnivores. Their favorite restaurants specialize in rats." Illary translated for us: "The Director says you are warmly welcomed; he adds that you have your chopsticks upside down." (Miss Oh: "Oh!") No.1 Frenchman posed a rhetorical question: "What is the Chinese attitude to the Big Noses? They find us outlandish."

Then to the airport, to take the fast jet to Xishuangbanna. Approaching our destination, Jing Hong (Daybreak City), we could see the yellow Mekong River issuing from its gorge, flowing through a country that, I fancied, resembled the Blue Ridge Mountains planted with rubber trees. In due course, officials of the state farm revealed their thinking. "In the rain forest the poets' hearts are full of enthusiasm and love for the flying bees and the dancing butterflies. But the beautiful rubber trees could not be found. So whole tracts were planted to rubber trees, which every seven years die from frost. [Oops! Chairman Mao made a booboo.] Therefore rubber plantations must revert to kingdom of plants and animals, with Amazing Scenery and Places of Historical Interest. And must be other business, too, tourist hotels and so on, to make profits." With these guidelines, we were conducted through a succession of forests and arboretums. "You will use your eyes to see these leaves," commanded Illary. In the adjoining fields Happy Peasants bobbed up and down, reaping and threshing. They resembled a large aerobics class. We passed a stylish young woman wearing a broad conical hat while deftly piloting a buffalo hitched to a plow.

Illary: (to the Frenchmen): What are you two talking about?
No. 1 Frenchman (rashly): We are talking about love.
Miss Oh (shocked): Oh!
Illary: That is for your private agenda.
Me: Miss Illary, we have now been here ten days. Each day we spend five hours feasting, in countless restaurants with names like Huge Wild Goose Bar. The rest of the time we blunder into nameless forests in search of "120

species of bamboo and two thousand orchids." I shall be dismissed as a consultant to Hyper Bank for failing to compile a list of loan requests.

Illary: I know you better than anyone else. What are you trying to say?

Me: I am happy under your direction.

Illary: If there is anything else you want, tell me. Now I will sing you a song, the most popular in China:

> *I love the national minorities*
> *They have lived here a long time*
> *They are very happy!*
> *They welcome people from overseas!*

Me (impelled to respond with a jingle of my own):

> *I love to travel with Hyper Bank!*
> *Sometimes we have a flat tire!*
> *Then the local people give us pineapple to eat!*

Illary: That is GREAT! Now tell me about the songs in America.
Me: I regret to say that there is a popular song, now current, that goes like this; and I proceeded to sing a few bars of a popular Country and Western ditty.
Miss Oh: (gasps) Oh!
Illary: I find this very disturbing.
Me: Would such a song be permitted on Chinese radio?
Illary: Of course not. Do *you* like this song?
Me: Of course not.
Illary: I think you have somewhat noble thoughts. This song is for the common people!

Information and inspiration lacking, our plan to transform the state farm lands (formerly prison farms) into profit centers was sketchy. All we had to show for our trouble was a pitifully short list of "opportunities" including, as I recall, tourist hotels and a fleet of busses whereby tourists could gawk at the aerobic peasants.

As with India many years before, I was baffled by China. So far my draft report read: "In the places we have visited, the people are happy and devoted to feasting. They admire natural scenery, and burst into song at every opportunity." That wouldn't do. I consulted No.1 Frenchman, who was never at a loss. No.1 was glad to explain, "There never was anything in China except a bit of silk, a little tea, and *a lot of cheap labor*. We – the West – thought China would be a market for our goods, but it turned out the other way around." So that's it, I thought. They've convinced the West to cannibalize our own industries by making it enormously profitable for Western businessmen to import from China. It's called "off-shore" manufacturing. Blame that old fake, Marco Polo, if you want to.

Somehow, I found time to visit the ancient temples in Beijing – places of which the airman Cecil Lewis wrote fondly (of his experiences in the 1920s) in his book *Sagittarius Rising*.)

What conclusions were drawn by the other five teams I was never told. But at the final meeting in Beijing the co-ordinator of the overall project, who was making heavy weather of assembling a mosaic of the Chinese "elephant" from the fragmentary reports she was getting, treated me with coldness. I couldn't help her. Building debt castles in the sand is an uncertain business. Then, while we were still struggling with our list of possible loans, the Director of State Farms arranged – at very short notice – a farewell banquet for us featuring a very large fondue pot full of boiling water, into which, the Frenchmen suggested, the Chinese (presumably frustrated by our lack of insight) might toss us one by one. I was only partially relieved to note alternative victuals, ready to serve the same office: a bowl of congealed pig's blood and a dish of snails. Then the *piece de resistance*, a massive tureen of soup, fortified with snake. "This is great!" said the Frenchmen in unison.

(Did I mention that from the first, I had suspected them of being deserters from the Foreign Legion?)

Illary: This is the happiest cuisine in the world!

Me: (affecting black humor): I would rather die than eat this.

Illary: You are joking, of course.

Me: I am eager to devour the smoked fish.

Englishman: I wish I were home. (Looks at photo of his pet rabbit.)

No. 2 Frenchman (the tourism expert): What do you do with the leftover food?

Ilary: I am sorry. I will order some more.

24

LAZY EIGHTS

After I landed my floatplane on the Pacific Coast on 7/25/1990, I turned my attention to other things. We moved to the country, to Madison County, Virginia, where I occupied myself pleasantly enough fixing up a small horse farm and consulting on behalf of a firm in Baton Rouge, LA. My assignments included a trip to Africa (where I got the short end of a lunch with the King of the Zulus) and trips to Angola (both the country of that name and the Louisiana State Prison, where I saw a memorable rodeo) and back to Central America.

Any sort of flying after my coast to coast adventure would be an anti-climax. Before I knew it, ten years had slipped by. The agent for getting me back into flying was our next-door neighbor, Glenn Lohr. Glenn was a livestock farmer, a school bus driver, a piano tuner, and an all-around entertaining guy. If there was a great banging noise after dark, it was Glenn Lohr's bull butting an old lime spreader in the back field. "He's been acting strange, that bull," admitted Glenn one day. "He butted me down yesterday, but I got away. Mr. Winkelman, the Swede, down the road, was not so lucky. He was killed by his bull about six weeks ago." Just then Glenn was pre-occupied with cleaning his chimney. He attempted to do this by dropping a boulder down the chimney, where it stuck, so he called on the neighbors for help to get it out.

January, 2000. Normality reigned in Radiant, VA. "Nothing ever happens around here," groaned Kay, the postmistress, who had just ejected her good-for-nothing husband from the house (he was "begging and praying to come back"). The Anabaptists around the corner were preoccupied with their particular vision of the world. "Shorty" Lohr, the tall man who owned the country store, was loading his car for a home delivery. "Six bottles of wine and 24 beers every Friday. He (the customer) was drying out quite well until the government started sending him a monthly $506 disability check." Down the road a piece, Alan Spivey's three llamas were guarding his sheep from the local "pet" dogs. Other folks were watching TV while sitting astride saddles bought from Crawford's Saddlery. (According to Crawford, many of the saddles he sold were to people who didn't own horses.)

All was normal, I say, when neighbor Glenn shook everything up by flying over the county in a small Cessna airplane. "They'll fool you every time," said Carolyn, referring no doubt to the "Ballad of Darius Green and his Flying Machine." It turned out Glenn was flying on a student license. (As aeronautical theory was not his strong suit, he never attempted the written test.) When I next saw him in the P.O., he recounted that the previous week he had gotten a call to tune a piano in Bumpass, VA. He was short of time so he flew his plane there, to the local airport. The owner of the piano refused to believe that her tuner had arrived by air, so went with her husband and son to the airport to confirm the fact – something to amaze her friends and relations.

From my journal:

2/25/2000. Glenn Lohr stopped over on his tractor, and we stacked and burned a brush pile. Glenn urged me to renew my flying license at Orange. "Elmer Dyre is the man to see," he said.

3/4/2000. I went to Orange Airport first thing, at 9.00A, for a flight check with Elmer Dyre. Elmer is 75 years old, a small, soft-spoken Iowan. Everyone likes him. He has been flying continuously since 1941, when he bought a "Waco low-wing" (whatever that was?) powered by a WW1-vintage 0X-5 engine "turning a 9' 3" dia. prop at 1450 RPM." Elmer is proud to call himself a "stick and rudder man," who advocates flying with a minimum amount of aileron. It was a beautiful day. We practiced "lazy eights" and chandelles.

3/13/2000. More lazy eights and chandelles with Elmer. A "Lazy 8" gets its name from the airplane's flight path as it traces a figure eight in the vertical plane when viewed from the side, and "S"-shaped when viewed from above.

3/18/2000. 11.00A. Sunny and 37F. Cold enough that I wore long under-wear. Flew to Manassas Airport on a check ride with Elmer. Returned to Orange at sunset – great view of Blue Ridge Mountains.

3/19/2000. Flew in Orange airport pattern with Elmer while weather dete-riorated. Then he signed me off, and we all went home.

4/5/2000. Glenn wanted to move his airplane from Louisa Airport to Gor-donsville (where he would get free tie-down in return for mowing the grass), and asked me to fly it there for him, as he would be busy with his bus route and his farm chores. It was only a 15-minute flight but it was memorable. All day the wind blew hard but at sunset the wind dropped, and I was able to taxi out to the takeoff runway. There was a big wild turkey, a gobbler, standing in the grass at the end of the runway. I took off to the west, and turned over the little town of Louisa, and followed the railroad tracks to Gordonsville, with the sky all to myself. Arriving over the airstrip, which is butted against Merry Mountain, I circled the field and descended steeply to land with full flaps and 60 kts on the clock. Glenn was waiting for me, nervous for his airplane I suppose. We tied the plane down and drove home in the dusk.

6/15/2000. Another pesky work trip, this one to Ethiopia. Left Cairo and flew down the Nile, past Khartoum, and then, after about three hours, arrived over Addis in the dark. Circled about forty-five minutes while the

Ethiopians tried unsuccessfully to get the runway lights working, then returned to Cairo, 1,500 miles back. Returned to Addis next day, went to hotel. Soon found myself locked in lavatory; called for help through window, hotel staff brought a scaling ladder and came in through French window and released me. From Addis, a large squalid city with goats and donkeys in the streets, drove seven hours west across a rolling upland plain. Reaching the escarpment, we had a splendid view of the Finchaa valley and sugar estate. The estate, at 37.25E, 09.45N employs 900 men to scare away the black-and-white colobus monkeys from eating the sugar cane. Significantly, they have to dump the molasses because, in this starving country, "there is no market."

7/29/2000. To New York City with Carolyn for tenth wedding anniversary trip. Nice trip, despite delayof 80 minutes on runway threshold due to unexpected visit of a bigwig to Manhattan on a shopping trip. (Rats!)

9/22/2000. I responded to an ad for a skydive pilot at Orange, to fly C-182. Charlie Snyder, FBO at Orange, emphatically discouraged me. "They want a jump pilot! It's strenuous work – on the edge!" I thought, at sixty-five years old, I don't get no respect! (I remembered Ginger Lacey, who was old at thirty-six.)

9/28/2000 and 9/29/2000. Flying practice at Orange.

10/12/2000. Columbus Day. I flew solo 5.5 hrs into the mountains to Beckley, WV and over the New River. The New River flows East to West – goes the "wrong way" across the Appalachians. (The river is older than the uplifted mountains.) I could see the direction of flow from the white water rapids.

10/13/2000. Today's task was to fly Glenn's plane for its annual inspection by a supposedly lenient mechanic at Hummel Airport on the Chesapeake Bay and return the same day. I was on the road before sunrise, in the light of the full moon. But when I got to the airport the engine wouldn't start. The plugs were frosted up and there was no hangar where the airplane could warm. (Glenn later bemoaned this failure – which he perceived to be mine – when the same airplane failed its inspection at Culpeper.)

10/19/2000. Glenn asked me to take his plane for inspection at Culpeper, because he had to drive the school bus, and substitutes were not available, i.e. it was easier to get a substitute pilot than to get a substitute bus driver. Anyway, I left home in the dark that morning and drove the 33 miles to Louisa, started the engine and flew the airplane to Culpeper Airport. And once in the air, flying solo, I had the realization again that the act of flight is a triumph. Today was sunny, after two days of rain and fog, and there was a lot of airport traffic because small airplanes, like bees and butterflies, come out on sunny days. Then Elmer showed up in a Beechcraft Baron. He was instructing the proud new owner of this bird, and had landed for a smoking break. So there was Elmer: old, diminutive, modest, likeable, greeted by everyone – all of us glad to know him.

Meanwhile the mechanic concluded that Glenn's airplane couldn't pass inspection without three or four items being corrected. It would cost $1300. Glenn, who had saved his first nickel, was aghast. While waiting for Glenn to pick me up, I chatted with the mechanic about flying. He told me he likes the Navion airplane. (Later I heard that his father, a dentist in Manassas, had crashed his Navion and killed himself, his wife, and two friends).

10/21/2000. I had reserved a Cessna airplane to fly Phyllis to Accomac, but she says she is now "scared of planes," so I cancelled the airplane and drove her as far as the Jefferson Hotel in Richmond where she got a ride from a friend. Driving back, at Gordonsville Airport, four F-18 fighter jets gave me a jolt as they thundered by at 200 feet altitude. This is an official "low fly" route. (Phyllis, you're right to be scared.)

10/24/2000. To Washington, DC to the Armenian Embassy on R Street, to hand in my visa application. (I'm going on another sugar mill study). Then, hopped into a cab to go to the National Gallery. The middle-aged immigrant driver was handling the cab like a fighter pilot; as I buckled my shoulder belt, we swerved onto Constitution Avenue and pulled up in front of the East Wing.

11/18/2000. Drive to outskirts of Yerevan and see Mt. Ararat. It is a magnificent sight, rising to 17,000 ft. from a flat plain. An American pilot, a fundamentalist Christian, says he has seen and photographed the remains of Noah's ark on its upper reaches. But the Armenians stuck to the business at hand. I was told, "We need to rebuild our sugar factory after the quake, so that we are not poisoned by the Muslim sugar imports."

1/20/2001. It was a cold day for the President's inauguration, and the bigwigs, all hatless, made a faintly ridiculous impression instead of the dynamic, youthful one they were presumably seeking.

2/7/2001. Flew lazy eights and chandelles with Elmer. He demonstrated the stability of the Cessna 172 by throttling right back and descending at 60 knots – hands off – with full flaps and the elevators trimmed full back.

Don the mechanic (who looks like Zero Mostel the actor) told me, "An airplane owner from New England brought me his airplane log books. 'How much do you charge for signing off the annual inspection?' he asked. 'Where's the plane?' I said. 'Oh, do you need to see it?' he asked."

3/8/2001. A fine morning, so I drove to Orange Airport without calling ahead. There was a plane available for me to rent, and I made six takeoffs and landings. Charge was $28.20. No-one else was flying.

3/14/2001. Last night wind buffeted the house, and this morning the wind persisted. But it was a sunny day so I stopped off at the airport after breakfast. The wind indicator showed 270 degrees, 14 knots, gusting to 24 knots. Elmer agreed to go up with me, and after a couple of practice landings we flew to Radiant and practiced "turns around a point" above my place, which shows off very nicely with the red roofs on the house, barn and out-buildings.

3/19/2001. Sunday morning I flew to Lynchburg and landed at tiny Fal-well Airport where you land uphill and takeoff downhill, regardless of wind direction. A fun trip.

3/21/2001. Stopped to see neighbor Sallie who, at age ninety, is a happy relic of the Jazz Age and indulges herself daily, smoking and drinking while watching "The Young and the Restless." She is well-pleased with her life, and recalls whole chapters of it in a Niagara of words. (Her son Dixon was killed in an Air Force jet training accident in 1964.)

3/28/2001. Sunny, 30F. Elmer helped me get the cold engine started, and I took off at 8.55A, turning right towards Fork Mountain, clearly visible 25 miles away. I planned to fly the Fairfax Line, the 1746 survey line connect-ing the sources of the Rappahannock and the Potomac rivers (the "Northern Neck"). I landed back at Orange at 11.00A, having completed a 200-mile flight over rugged country in two hours. Soon I was sitting in a local café, with coffee and burger. I was thinking: "This was a perfect flight. I got to pick one of the best days of the month; flew solo, low over remote places, navigating with map and compass."

4/26/2001. Glenn Lohr's Cessna was now at Bumpass, at Lake Louisa Air-port, I don't know why, and he wanted me to fly him to Bumpass in a rented airplane from Orange. I got to Orange, removed the starling's nest from under the cowling, and refueled the airplane. But the right brake wasn't holding, so I drove Glenn to Bumpass, along the empty country roads, past little churches and the dogwood in bloom. It was a beautiful day with a sharp little wind.

6/09/2001. I finally got to fly in the yellow Piper Cub at Orange Airport – not with Elmer; he's sick and run down. The instructor taxied and flew the airplane with exaggerated care, and informed me that twenty-five hours dual instruction was a perquisite to solo. But we spent a delightful twenty min-utes in the air, doing simple maneuvers over the deep green woods.

7/12/2001. I went to the airfield this morning and got the keys for a C-150 and found it was empty of fuel. Seems that last night a student was doing some solo flying "in the pattern" under Elmer's supervision – just a couple of circuits before dark. Well, the student decided to do some sight-seeing, and soon became lost. He radioed that he was "over some lakes," then: "I think I'm over Charlottesville." It was now quite dark. He was deaf to Elmer's advice to home in on the VOR, and soon lost the channel and was out of touch. Another airplane was dispatched to look for him, but no luck. Over an hour passed, and Elmer was getting ready to call the Civil Air Patrol to report a missing airplane. Then the 150 appeared, very low, and landed back at Orange. It was 10.30P. The student was surprised to find himself at Orange (and had never made a night landing before). Elmer told me, "In 8,000 hours of instruction, I have never been so concerned." After the "lost" airplane was refueled, I went up for an hour's flying.

9/11/2001. I was drinking a cup of tea and idly watching TV, which was reporting a dishwasher recall. I copied down the relevant serial numbers and went and confirmed that our dishwasher was not affected. Carolyn said, "Come look at the TV. There's some sort of report that an airplane just collided with one of the towers of the World Trade Center." Then, in real time, we watched amazed as another jetliner crashed into the other tower, about two-thirds of the way up from the ground. The image was endlessly repeated. Two jetliners had flown into the Twin Towers, one into each tower, one after the other. I thought, "Palestine." It seemed to be the footage of a far-off event, but a biblical event. Now tiny figures were leaping from one of the towers, falling like dolls to the ground below.

10/15/2001. Across the road, on Glenn's place, a Mennonite was flying a powered parachute from a little rolling meadow. This flying machine is a trike ultralight, powered by a 65 HP Rotax 2-cylinder, water-cooled engine. Before take-off the operator laid the parachute out on the ground and checked that the lines were not tangled. Then he started the engine by pulling a toggle, the propeller revved up, and the contraption rolled forward in no time, as the parachute inflated, and the machine climbed into the air. "If I had that machine," said an onlooker, a tractor mechanic, admiringly, "I'd keep going up and never come down."

The trike's owner doesn't have a pilot license and has never flown a conventional airplane. I told neighbor Bill, "The powered parachute flies at 26 mph and is very noisy. Our dog starts barking even before it appears over the trees."

11/20/2001. The big news in Madison is that the Wrangler jeans plant (here fifty years) is closing with the loss of 238 scarce jobs. This RIF is supposedly justified by the company's target of "14 percent operating margin." Off they go, to Mexico. But they will still sell all their output in the USA. (Of course!) One of our neighbors stopped by. She is about to lose her job at a local fabric manufacturer (they're going to Mexico, too). Juanita heard the president of the factory openly bragging about the several big houses he owns, and of his wife's expensive jewelry – "all in front of $10/hour employees." She said her daughter-in-law works for a national charity and that her boss expects her to do most of the work "for peanuts."

12/7/2001. Stopped on the way home at a new barber and got my third haircut this week, in an attempt to correct the first two, administered by a barber nicknamed "kicked-in-the-head," who was kicked in the head by a horse at the age of ten.

4/7/2002. Flying with Elmer (2.2 hrs). Day was cold, windy, sunny and bumpy. I did some instrument practice "under the hood," including recovery from unusual attitudes. After that, a hammerhead – and then I felt queasy. There was a lot of static on the headphones, and I couldn't hear what Elmer was saying half the time. The heat was turned up, thick smelly heat. I wanted to throw up, but I had nothing in my stomach but cornflakes. Elmer was very chipper – smoked a cigarette and "signed me off".

4/11/2002. Eight landings with Elmer at Orange. The wind veered and picked up speed, so I got some cross-wind landing practice.

4/13/2002. Flying with Elmer. He said he only feels good when he is flying; otherwise, not so good. He took up my offer to drive to the store to bring him a pack of cigarettes.

4/25/2002. Fog and drizzle scrubbed my planned visit to daughter Phyllis in Onancock. This was the only day I could get on Elmer's schedule but the weather turned bad – though it was a fine day yesterday, and the next day also. (I'm not currently checked out on any airplane, so need to take Elmer along.) In a pasture on Lost Mountain, I saw a mare with a foal.

5/5/2002 Elmer was not at the airport. He'd been injured in the crash of his airplane, I found later. ("The engine quit on take-off for undetermined reasons.")

I didn't know that at the time, only knew he'd been feeling poorly. Drove to Louisa today and tried out their Cessna 172, a hangar queen "not to be used for touch-and-goes." It was Sunday and the parachutists were out. "These guys are all crazy. They don't announce their jumps; then they land all over: on the runway, in town and – two weeks ago – right through the hangar roof." I flew for one hour, checking out the radios. Then I reserved the plane for tomorrow, 10:00A – 4:00P.

5/6/2002. Today I flew over to Accomack Airport, stayed three hours, and got back to Louisa by 4.00P. It's a great feeling, flying solo over the forests, fields, and rivers – all laid out on a generous scale – with roads, cars, towns, and people barely noticeable. Instead of driving two hundred tiresome miles of congested road along a U-shaped route via Norfolk, I flew direct, easily, relaxed, across the Bay. I've flown to Accomack a dozen times before, but I'd forgotten how good it feels in the air. I could have navigated by GPS and flown on automatic pilot. But I preferred to fly by compass and land-marks, as though I were flying the Tiger Moth. I flew over King's Dominion

Amusement Park, and over the bridges across the Mattaponi River and the mouth of the Rappahannock River on my way to the Eastern Shore. And no-one else in the sky! (Except for a fish-spotting plane below me, a scout for the Menhaden fleet.) Phyllis met me at the airport in a red convertible, looking very stylish in a black dress with vintage hat and handbag. (She is staying in the port of Onancock.)

10/9/2002. No flying because Orange A/P operator gave up, complaining that insurance premiums had gone too high. It has come out that the terrorists who hijacked the jetliners and crashed them into the Twin Towers had received pilot training at small, unregulated airports in Florida, so all small plane operators are closely watched.

4/5/2003. I heard from Glenn that Elmer died in March. He never fully recovered from his airplane crash at Louisa the previous April. Air traffic at Orange tailed off. There was no-one to take Elmer's place.

Now I hear that Glenn and two pals plan to base their three flying machines (Glenn's ultralight plus the powered parachute and a friend's gyrocopter) on Glenn's little meadow. Now, there's a flying circus for you!

25

TWEEDLE DEE & TWEEDLE DUM

10/13/2001. With Elmer gone, Orange Airport activity was at a low ebb, so I drove the 22 miles to Charlottesville Airport to see Dick Yates, who runs a flight school there.

"Who've you been flying with?"
"Elmer Dyre."
"Well, that's OK."

It was just about sunset, 5.00P, when we walked out to the flight line. After fussing over the plane a while, we taxied out and took off to the north. Ascending into the air, the view expanded exponentially; the landscape rose up around us. The air was still, the woods were copper, the western sky beyond the Blue Ridge was flaming red. The airplane rose easily, serenely, several thousand feet into the air. We did a few maneuvers, and turned back to the airport (all we could see of it was the flashing beacon). We made two circuits and landings in the twilight (too dark to read the flight instruments) and taxied in at six o'clock.

11/01/2003. Another gorgeous fall day. I'm back for more flying with Dick. The driver of the refueling truck, an elderly black man, greeted me. "I know you," he said, "We're Glenn's neighbors." Harold has pumped gas at the airport for forty years, and now works part time. He is less than spry, but very genial; a bit of a comic character (aren't we all?), quite out of place among the sleek jet planes that are parked there. (One of them is a $40 million Dassault long-range executive transport.) Amid these shiny airplanes, Harold confided that he is helping Glenn "look for some nuts and bolts for his ultralight." In the same earnest tone, he added, "Glenn has his plane tied down with baling twine. It's not going to hold with any kind of wind."

11/06/2003. Second day of rain, 2 1/2 inches in all. This was not predicted in advance and spoiled my flying and the hay-making of Glenn's brother, Harrison, who says he has no hay for our horses. Then he confided that he was having trouble with his 37-year old girlfriend, whom, he noted, was not well suited as she didn't have a job, was fond of the bottle, and expected too much of him.

11/07/2003. I flew off the big runway at Charlottesville and attempted to land at nearby Gordonsville, whose runway is a third of the length and a third of the width of the runway at Charlottesville. Result: I overshot and had to try a second time. But it was fun. PS. This Skyhawk has a high-lift wing.

11/08/2003. I planned to fly to Hot Springs Airport, on top of the mountain there, and at the last minute asked Fitz if he wanted to go. It was gusty at Charlottesville, and Fitz, an instructor at the airport, thought it would be too windy in the mountains, but in fact the wind was reported at only five knots at Hot Springs Airport, which is at 3800 feet elevation. Flying there at 6500 feet and 110 knots, the scenery of mountain ridges, passes and valleys made a wonderful sight. We landed on the table top mountain for a cup of coffee, and then made a second landing. (One for me, and one for him.)

11/15/2003. Today I flew down to Hampton Roads airport to see Phyllis and Lucas. It was all so simple, so direct, so effortless. This is how the aviation age was supposed to be, when a handful of companies built all those little airplanes in 1947. One was supposed to take off from his local airport, fly direct to the town he wanted to visit, and land there at the local airport to be met by his daughter or aunt or whomever was the object of the visit.

On this particular visit, I went aboard Lucas's 30-ton ketch *Kiva*, in which he had crossed the Atlantic twice.

11/20/2003. Flew to Manassas, only seventy miles away, and found that it is now an Air Defense Identification Zone (ADIZ), requiring a flight plan and lots of in-flight reporting. The ether was thick with the jabbering of pilots and the petulant chiding of controllers. This spoiled what was otherwise a beautiful Indian summer day.

12/02/2003. I flew to Kitty Hawk in a C172, prompted by the upcoming centenary of the Wright Bros first flight. It was a bright, cold day with the wind gusting out of the northwest at 17 knots or more. I took off from Charlottesville, wrestling with wind on takeoff, and turned downwind to set course at 10.15A. About noon I arrived over the Outer Banks, and circling over the runway at Kitty Hawk, I looked around at the long, thin sandbank. Fully exposed to the ocean waves, it is now built over with houses. There were white horses on the sea. As there was no fuel at Kitty Hawk, I flew to the nearby Coast Guard airfield at Elizabeth City. The wind was reported as "330/12 knots gusting to 22", and I brought my plane in over the Pasquotank River, descending to land on Runway 28. (This expansive moment – the big runway ahead, the sparkling river below, the overarching blue sky – somehow registered as the dominant impression of the day, elbowing aside all others.)

After two hours on the ground at Elizabeth City, I took off to the northwest, passing over the small, rectangular harbor – the water streaked by wind lines – in the centre of town. Visibility was at least sixty miles. Off to the right were the white office towers of Norfolk. Here was the power of flight – the power of movement (something that the automakers try daily, vainly, to conjure up in their advertisements); but I would fly from the sea coast to the high mountains of the Blue Ridge in just an hour or so, rotating the earth as I wished by a movement of the controls; seeing besides, with a perspective that no motorist can see, that inland from the sea Virginia consists not of congested highways and shopping malls, but of a few big rivers and endless acres of forest. Approaching the Blue Ridge, I aimed at the gap in the low front range of hills and landed at Charlottesville in a gusty crosswind (330/12 G20). By the time I left the airport for home, the short winter day was already ending.

12/18/2003. Yesterday, on the one hundredth anniversary of powered flight, President Bush and 40,000 spectators gathered at Kitty Hawk to watch an exact replica of the Wright Flyer attempt to fly. It couldn't do it. There was no wind.

12/20/2003. Outside the library at UVA, I stopped to see Borglum's statue of a winged Icarus commemorating James McConnell, a student who enlisted in the Lafayette Escadrille and was shot down March 19, 1917 flying a Nieuport biplane. (Some of the frat boys have contended that the statue is an eyesore. God knows who they world have built a statue to? Themselves? Certainly the legions of Icarus sculptures and of cemetery monuments of angels in human form, all underestimate the very large wing area necessary for muscle-powered flight.)

12/28/2003. Flew to Hampton Roads (1.5 hours) on a gorgeous day. The wind was calm, and I came in rather fast and bounced. Lunched in Portsmouth with Phyllis and Lucas and others.

1/7/2004. Very cold and windy. But I had arranged to take Tweedle Dee and Tweedle Dum flying – a date postponed once because of the wind. TDum and TDee, brothers-in-law, both retired, live together on our road; they sometimes snowplow our driveway. Today they arrived at the appointed hour of 8.30A, driving an oversized SUV and bundled up like two astronauts. When we got to the airport the two Tweedles (short and stout, something like a Tenniel drawing) waited in the lounge, ogling the svelte Learjet passengers, while our airplane's engine was pre-heated. Tweedle Dum would go first. I got him in the front seat, with the seat belt adjusted tightly, somewhere below his belly. Now I primed the engine and pumped the throttle. But I flooded the engine. We disembarked while Dick Yates got it going again (that took ten minutes). Then I flew TDum up into the ether, the airplane rocking in the wind. TDum, I noticed, was clutching the door handle, grimacing the while. "Are you O.K.?"

"I've always had a fear of heights."

"Look, it's safer than driving a car," I said, taking my hands off the control yoke but flying very smoothly. "You can see by the dials that we're at three thousand feet, doing a hundred knots. And those little bumps you feel are only the wind blowing across the hills." But Tweedle Dum was not to be mollified. It was such a long way to fall. (This was contagious. I felt a passing twinge of anxiety as I stared straight down at the wooded hillsides far, far below, perhaps remembering that I had had a parachute when flying air force planes and gliders.) After circling once over his house, we returned to the airport and landed in the crosswind. "I think Stu (TDee) will want to wait for a better day," said TDum.

TDee agreed. He would wait for another day.

"At least I'll show you the plane," I offered.

Well, Tweedle Dee liked the plane & the gadgets therein. "I think I'd like to go up," he said. Once in the air, Tweedle Dee, whose third airplane ride in a lifetime this was, was entranced with the prospect from the sky. And why not? The sun shone on the Blue Ridge Mountains as we soared over the rivers and roads and towns of this part of the Piedmont. "There's Ruckersville!" called TDee. "And Luck Stone Quarry!"

When he got down, he talked to Dick about taking flying lessons.

As a commentary on the wonderful adaptability of Americans, Tweedle Dee, a retired dental technician looking to supplement his income, got himself a commercial driver's license last year and took a job as a solo trans-continental trucker. He did a spell in California, "driving down the long grade of the

Donner Pass, pumping his air brakes." (Tweedle Dee is very short. Carolyn wonders how he reaches the pedals.) Tweedle Dum, a retired police officer, equally short of cash, was less adventurous. He got a job as security officer in a local warehouse.

3/26/2004. Flew to Hampton Roads to pick up Robbie. The airport was a zoo, with pilots landing in any direction they wanted. A visiting pilot brazenly landed her twin-engine Mitsubishi downwind. We thought she had "bought the farm" but she braked heavily, taxied in, and peremptorily ordered "fill 'er up." (She was en route to Florida). Robbie and I had a wonderful flight to Onancock and return, with an un-matched view of Norfolk, Newport News and Hampton. We had very good communications with Norfolk Approach Control.

4/29/2004. Avoided cutting our grass by going flying. Flew over the mountain to Eagles Nest and made two landings on that short runway.

[I quit flying for a while.]

2/24/2005. Dave Browning came around in his bib overalls and fixed our clothes dryer. On a day like this, he recalled, his repair truck flipped on the ice and skidded upside down into a creek. The local wrecker pulled out Dave's truck, and she started right up. "There wasn't a scratch on it." (Dave's voice hits a high pitch when he's making a point.) Dave, have you thought of taking flying lessons?

2/25/2005. To the airport before noon. I planned to fly to Lynchburg but the clouds didn't lift until 1.30P and then were barely fifteen hundred feet above ground. So I went with Dick Yates to practice Lazy Eights over I-64, on the other side of the Southwest Mountains, through the Shadwell Gap.

3/01/2005. Carolyn backed out of a plan to drive through wintry weather to Bluefield, WV, for a business meeting with a prospective client tomorrow. Her two gung-ho colleagues insisted on flying there from Dulles.

(I checked the forecast for Bluefield Airport; it was at minimums, with visibility forecast at one statute mile.) The intrepid colleagues ended up on a plane to Charleston, WV, in turbulent air, with many of their fellow passengers throwing up their breakfasts. There was more vomiting on the ensuing night-time taxi drive through the mountains to Bluefield.

3/03/2005. Captured: a perfect day for flying. It was clear, cold (-2C), windy. I dressed warmly and drove to Charlottesville Airport. There was a hard outline to the snow-covered Blue Ridge Mountains. I made a two-hour flight as far as the Rappahannock and York Rivers and back NW to Charlottesville. From my turning point at 5,000 feet over West Point I could see the Eastern Shore across Chesapeake Bay. Soon after that the Blue Ridge Mountains came in sight, 80 miles in my direction of flight. This was a day to say, I like winter flying, I like Virginia, and I like Charlottesville Airport.

3/08/2005. Weather report of wind at Kill Devil Hill clocked at 110 mph.

3/18/2005. Flew my favorite cross-country: Charlottesville – Lynchburg/Falwell – Hot Springs Airport – Charlottesville. I was thinking: "Flying this route regularly, alternated with a X-C across the Bay, say to Crisfield, would keep me happy for a long time."

4/28/2005. A fine, sunny day, though a bit windy. Flew to the small airport at Williamsburg for lunch. The aerial perspective is very different from an approach in a car down I-64. From the airplane south of Richmond I could see, thirteen miles ahead, the tiny but obvious scar of the airstrip alongside the James River.

5/10/2005. Took off at 9.00A to embrace a peerless morning and the entirety of fields, forests and mountains. I climbed to 5,000 feet, crossed the mountain ridge and descended to land at Shenandoah airport for breakfast. What a wonderful "back yard!" Back over Charlottesville, tuning in the landing frequency, I noticed that I was circling high over Monticello.

26

KNUCKLEBUSTER
(AN AIRPLANE WITH
A STRONG PERSONALITY)

2/18/2004. Cold, bright morning; dog's water bucket frozen again. Faced with an uninspiring list of chores at home, I drove to the Charlottesville airport & thence flew to Orange to practice landings. The wind was gusty, 8 – G20, twirling the yellow windsock around its pole and making landing a bit of an adventure. I drove home feeling pretty good.

2/23/2004. Phoned Jim Buckley, who is in Peachtree City, a suburb of Atlanta, about flying his North American SNJ-5, a Navy version of the Texan/Harvard that I flew fifty years ago in 1954. (I was on the next-to-last course in the RAF to train on the Harvard.) He said the week of March 1 to 5 would be convenient for him.

2/24/2004. There is no cheap and easy way to get to Atlanta. Driving is too tedious. There is a direct flight from Charlottesville to Atlanta, but the price is excessive, $700. A sleeper birth on the train is too expensive, and going by bus entails a twenty-hour ride. Dick Yates said, "Take one of our planes. It's only a two-and-a-half hour flight." Yes, but even if that were true, the weather at this time of year, a few weeks from spring, is generally unsettled. Besides, there are two separate weather arcas to consider – Atlanta and Virginia/Carolinas.

2/26/2004. Day number six with head cold. I bought the sectional charts at the airport and took them home to work out the best route to Atlanta. (At the Charlottesville airport, saw a stylish airplane, a Piaggo twin-engine, with five-bladed props.)

2/28/2004. Flew Dick's Skyhawk to Peachtree, a sunny 4.7 hour trip along the east edge of the Appalachians, with one stop – at snowy Hickory, N.C. A bit of a circus at Hickory, with the radio full of chatter with two planes reporting themselves lost. "I run out of gas," said a heavily accented voice. "I must go down!" (Twenty minutes later I encountered this same actor – a Serb? – in the flight office, nothing amiss.) Passed by Mt. Mitchell, 6684 feet, and the monadnock of Pilot Mountain.

I dog-legged around Atlanta metro area to Falcon/Peachtree Airport. Navigation, by GPS, was a breeze: just dial in the airport code and follow directions. Noted: massive Stone Mountain, near Atlanta. Then Peachtree/Falcon, a single tarmac strip surrounded by pine trees.

2/29/2004. Met up with Jim Buckley at the Confederate Air Force hangar. He sized me up. I was older than he'd expected. In the A.M., I familiarized myself with the cockpit controls, which I guess you could characterize as "Hollywood, 1940." In the P.M., we got into the air but only after lengthy taxi practice, creeping around the apron and along the runway in serpentine fashion in order to see around the big nose. This plane must be tamed on the ground as well as in the air. Sharp turns on the ground require unlocking the tail wheel.

From my notes: "Now for takeoff. The view ahead, even from the front cockpit, is poor. The propeller torque pulls the airplane to the left, so right rudder is required. So far, so good. But the ergonomics of moving the undercarriage and flap levers in the SNJ are bad! The landing gear lever is low down, forward on the left. To raise the wheels involves reaching forward and pulling the spring-loaded, red-painted knob (looks like a valve on an old-fashioned radiator) up and forward to release it from its groove, then up and back to its next (gear up) niche. That done, one presses down on the hydraulic power button. Once airborne, I couldn't move the lever at all, and my struggles caused the airplane to pitch up and down. Over the radio: "Hey, flyboy! Got your finger in your ass?" (No control tower here: pilots hot rod around, cutting in on each other, landing in any direction they like, and so forth.) Another thing: I had to release my safety harness in order to move forward in the seat to reach the gear lever knob. On subsequent flights I worked out the following procedure: (1) Unlock the harness – I didn't tell Jim this, (2) brace yourself for the effort, (3) *wrench* the red knob out of its niche & pull it back, (4) move left hand back & press down on hydraulic button, (5) verify gear position by checking the mechanical indicators in cockpit, and by looking out of the cockpit at the indicators in the wing roots."

"With wheels up, which should be effected immediately after takeoff, reduce the engine power, throttle and pitch, and fly the airplane in a climbing turn to get on the downwind leg. Now reduce the power again and put the wheels down (comparatively easy) for the landing. Next the flaps: (1) press the hydraulic button, (2) *slap the flap lever hard*, back to the down position, (3) *snatch* the lever forward again, back to the neutral position, before the flaps go too far down, e.g. to forty degrees when you only need twenty." But the quadrant for the spring-loaded flap lever has sharp edges, so by this time my left knuckles were bleeding profusely. (They didn't call these old airplanes "knucklebusters" for nothing. I had a pain in my left shoulder, too, from working the landing gear lever. I didn't admit to myself that maybe I didn't have the muscular strength anymore.)

I've gone into detail on the flap and landing gear levers because working them was very distracting. I don't recall any such problem flying the Harvard fifty years ago (or in flying the P-51 fifteen years ago). But in purchasing the Harvard – many of which were manufactured under license in Montreal – the RAF specified modifications to these particular controls. The airplane I flew at Peachtree, though, an SNJ-5, was built at Inglewood, CA, for the U.S. Navy.

In the air, the J-Bird is light on the controls, and responsive to the rudder. With its tail wheel configuration, the airplane – like all tail draggers – is directionally unstable, as they were expected to take off and land into the wind. Hence, they were normally operated from airfields with three intersecting runways, such as Moreton-in-Marsh, where I trained. Another thing: the SNJ/Harvard, having twice the weight of the average light airplane, is more likely to bounce on landing. On the third bounce, you need to "go around again."

After bandaging my knuckles, and buying a pair of kid-skin gloves, I was ready for the next morning's session.

3/1/2004. But the wind was blowing hard this Monday morning, the first day of March. This afternoon a pilot told me that landing a Boeing 737 in a crosswind at Atlanta that morning had been "quite a handful." Jim's advice to me was to sit some more in the SNJ cockpit and "really get to know it." (To think that at one time I knew the cockpit well enough to fly solo night cross-country flights.)

3/2/2004. Only one session today, because the wind was gusting to 24 mph.

The Dixie wing of the Confederate Air Force (recently renamed the Commemorative Air Force) is housed in a new hangar on the airport. Its collection includes a Douglas Dauntless torpedo bomber, a Bell King Cobra and other classic airplanes. The CAF was founded in Texas, in 1961. According to a plaque on the wall, the Dixie wing received its charter in 1989 from Jethro E. Culpeper.

Jim Buckley, my instructor, is a 16,000-hour airline pilot, currently co-pilot for a discount airline. "After my airline went bust, I went from $200,000 a year to a fraction of that." Jim is a great guy who doesn't say much; sometimes I wish he would. ("Yeah, y'could have put that wing down a bit sooner.")

3/3/2004. Two sessions today. Errors in landing the SNJ: failure to round out properly, landing with excess speed, & bouncing or ballooning. The SNJ is a frisky machine.

3/4/2004. Two more sessions, and I'm getting the hang of this machine. But Dick wants his Skyhawk back in Charlottesville this weekend, so I plan to leave tomorrow. I've completed eight hours, and twenty-six landings with the CAF at Peach Tree. Jim says his airline-pilot co-owner needed twenty hours to solo in the SNJ. (When I refer to my RAF log book, I see that I had seven and a half hours of dual before solo.) Now, I'd need fifteen hours to feel competent to take the SNJ round by myself (is this optimistic?) because of the awkward cockpit layout and the single runway. In the late 1940s the USAF retired its basic trainers and started cadet pilots, sink or swim, in the AT-6 Texan, which the student pilots were required to solo in <30 hours – or else!

3/5/2004. The weather forecast for the return flight was OK, so I checked out of the motel and turned my car in. I made one last check of the weather: "a fast approaching front is causing turbulence below ten thousand feet and high surface winds in a large area stretching east from Chattanooga to the Atlantic coast." I put my bags back in the car, and returned to the hotel.

3/6/2004. The weather charts were cluttered with computer-generated fronts from New England to Florida. But a friendly forecaster advised, on the phone, "The outlook for tomorrow on your route is good."

3/7/2004. I was at the airport at 6.30A. A full moon was high in the western sky, and a bright dawn in the east. I put my luggage in the Skyhawk, and phoned the flight service station to file my flight plan. A surly briefer (he'd evidently been vigorously stirring the entrails on his night watch) snarled, "Don't you realize the mountain tops in Virginia are obscured, and the visibility along the route you say you want to travel is five miles or less?" But the view out of the window was good, and I told the angry seer that I'd start by flying east of the direct route, away from the mountains. I took off and headed for Charlotte, NC. Ceiling and visibility were unrestricted – bore no relation to the computer-generated weather. But still, a fast-moving clipper front had been mooted, and I pushed Old Dobbin, the Skyhawk, along as fast as I could, 110 knots. After my struggles with the SNJ, flying a Skyhawk was like driving an automobile.

27

A FLIGHT IN A BALLOON

5/27/2005. Ballooning retains the unpredictability that has been so efficiently minimized in most other forms of human flight. After watching the weather Carolyn booked a flight on a balloon from the nearby Boar's Head Inn, in Charlottesville. Such flights leave at 6.30A – weather permitting. We were lucky to have a fine morning with light winds. The balloon, of 64,000 cubic feet, can lift ten persons, including the pilot, in a large wicker basket like a clothes hamper. (This particular wicker basket was made in Shropshire, England.) Like the very first Montgolfier balloon of 1783, our balloon will lift itself when the air in the canopy is heated. To effect this, the pilot operates a sort of Bunsen burner below the balloon canopy's orifice, thereby heating the air in the balloon and causing it to rise.

This morning, before inflating the balloon, the pilot released a small trial balloon which rose rapidly and flew away in a northeast direction. Apparently satisfied with the speed and direction of the wind, the pilot ordered that the main balloon be inflated and prepared for launch. The nine passengers clambered into the basket, and the balloon rose slowly into the air, proceeding at the speed of a bicycle across the north side of town and at heights of between 200 and 600 feet above the ground.

A sensation of stillness, caused by the lack of relative wind, is peculiar to ballooning, and seemed to me to contribute to a precariousness not evidenced in the more robust heavier-than-air version of flight. On this clear morning, the view of the surrounding mountains was superb. The city of Charlottesville looked better from the air than it did from the ground, with the added interest of intimate views such as a solitary jogger, and a stout woman walking out of the front door of her dilapidated house. We cruised low over the Rivanna River, seeing the reflection of our balloon in the water below us. There was a "whoosh" when the pilot goosed the Bunsen burner to gain height after we brushed through the tops of tulip poplar trees by the side of the river. We had close views of handsome houses and estates invisible from the road.

After three quarters of an hour, the pilot looked for a landing spot in this broken country. All the while he was in contact with the retrieval truck. He descended toward a small field and prepared to land, but thought better of it and goosed the Bunsen burner to gain height, and continued floating eastward. Ahead of us I could see a largish field on the corner of Route 20 and Proffit Road. I was surprised when our pilot descended short of this inviting field (ground access too difficult, I supposed) and landed in a tiny space between a cedar tree and a partly-built house. Simultaneously the truck arrived, and the driver took hold of a rope attached to the balloon. Five of us passengers were instructed to disembark and take hold of other ropes; then the pilot powered the balloon twenty feet into the air, and we on the ground pulled the floating balloon by ropes over the various obstacles in its path until we reached the roadside and the retrieval van and trailer.

At this point, an irate homeowner issued from his house across the road. While the huge balloon was deflated on his front lawn, he complained of our trespassing while telling us of all his troubles. (A mild reaction compared to that of the French peasants who attacked Montgolfier's balloon with pitchforks in their backyard 220 years ago.) Our pilot affected surprise at this reception. "This almost never happens", said he, implying that people on the ground welcome aerial intrusions. "They more often offer us champagne."

Meanwhile, inspection of my map showed that the wind had carried us at nine knots, in a direction of 077 degrees true, a trajectory that, if continued unchanged, would have taken us to the British Isles – or on to the Duchy of Nassau, where Monck Mason ended his wonderfully insouciant balloon trip, which had begun eighteen hours previously at Vauxhall Gardens beside the Thames in the year 1836.

Next day, I drove back to retrieve my jacket, which I had left in the balloon pilot's truck. When he emailed me the directions he omitted a crucial item, the name of his street. I knocked on the door of a house in the general vicinity to inquire. A woman, remarkably presentable, answered the door. She couldn't make sense of my directions. "He's the pilot for the balloon at the Boar's Head Inn," I said. She pointed the way to a run-down house at the end of a steep, descending drive. Ballooning evidently doesn't pay very well. (Today was the first time in three weeks that the balloon could get airborne.)

28

MODEL PLANES AGAIN

8/11/2005. Drove to a meeting of the Rivanna Model Airplane Club, a pleasant 30-mile drive along Routes 231 and 22 through pretty country. Milton Field is the former Charlottesville aerodrome (1940 – 1965), with its grass runways overgrown, except for the third, short runway now used by model airplanes. This land, in the flood plain of the Rivanna River, was formerly part of T. Jefferson's plantation, Shadwell. (His family came from the Shadwell area of London.)

I got the chance to pilot a radio-controlled Tiger Moth, and the promise of instruction "when this spell of summer heat abates." Drove home in the dark, the long way, on Routes 250 and 29, to avoid deer.

8/13/2005. Came across an article in the *NY Review of Books*, dated Nov. 2003, entitled "Tumult in the Clouds" (title borrowed from Yeats) by Roger Shattuck, celebrating the centenary of the Wright's first flight. The author, a prof from Boston University and former pilot, doesn't like airplanes much; he describes them as "elaborate prosthetic devices to transport us through the air." (But he praises Hopkins's poem, *The Windhover*.) The prof says writings on flight don't fly. There is no literature of flight, presumably because hyperbolic action hogs the whole tale at the expense of the human condition. (Even the action-packed *Iliad* hinges on the jealousy and resentment of Achilles.)

Richard Rumbold, in his biography of Antoine de Saint-Exupéry, *The Winged Life* (1952), anticipated Shattuck in asserting that "flying has inspired surprising little good writing." In his view flying signifies: first, ascent, endeavor, aspiration; and second, escape, release, freedom. Well, yes.

Surely there is some good writing on flight? The epic of flight, the myth of Daedalus, was written down some two thousand years ago. Is it the case that after a thousand years of leaping from towers, a hundred years of heavier-than-air flight, and an enormous amount of scribbling, that we are still waiting for a sequel to the Daedalus story?

I can think of twenty or more outstanding books on flight out of the several hundreds I've read; here are a dozen (not in any particular order):

> *Listen! The Wind* (Anne Morrow Lindbergh)
> *My Airships* (Santos-Dumont)
> *Where No Birds Fly* (Wills)
> *The High and the Mighty* (Gann)
> *West with the Night* (Markham)
> *Solo Flight* (Batten)
> *By the Seat of My Pants* (Smith)
> *Gods of Tin* (Salter)
> *Going Solo* (Dahl)
> *The Sky Beyond* (Taylor)
> *Night Flight* (Saint-Exupéry)

8/22/2005. To Shadwell on this hot day to get some instruction from Jim Price on flying radio-controlled airplanes. This was not entirely satisfactory, as the trainer he used had three axes of control, whereas the simpler models, like my Cub, have two axes (lacking ailerons). Also, we were using a "buddy box," which is a slave transmitter hooked to the master transmitter whereby he kept overriding my inputs so that I didn't know who was flying. At one time I had the trainer inverted. Then Jim test-flew my new Cub, which flew beautifully. Jim confided that the gated golfing community across the river complains to the University about "the noise model airplanes make on Sunday afternoons." Puts them off their stroke.

8/24/2005. A fine morning with Canadian air. Back to Shadwell flying field and succeeded in flying the model Cub under radio control (with neighbor Bill hand-launching the plane), though I crash-landed on each of four flights, with slight damage only. This was more fun than flying a full-size Skyhawk. Things happen faster! It's great fun to guide the little plane around the sky on its fast and twisting trajectory, something like a racing pigeon, and to try to bring her back to earth.

A few days later, flew my new model airplane, larger and slower than the Piper Cub, in my own back field. Even though I had had two tall pines felled, the space was still undersized (s/be 600 feet across). A puff of wind rendered the model airplane uncontrollable by radio control, and she stalled into the top of a tall tree. I paid Joe $60 to get the plane down. (Well, he did make a precarious climb and might, like Icarus, have fallen to the ground.)

29

THE IDEAL PROGRAM

We moved from our place in the country to a townhouse in Charlottesville, which was located in the flight pattern of the airport. That same week, on September 6, 2007, a low-time pilot from Brunswick, GA, crashed at night into Fork Mountain (elevation 3,845 ft). Someone was bound to do it, I suppose. (This landmark dominated our skyline for fourteen years, ever since we moved there.) The three occupants were looking for the airport at Winchester.

My last batch of flying in Virginia comprised seventy-five pleasure flights. These were to the airports at Shenandoah, Orange, Luray, Louisa, Farmville, Falwell/Lynchburg, Williamsburg, Richmond, Greenbriar and Tappahannock. My favorite destination was Falwell; landing uphill was a cheap thrill.

10/15/2007. To the airport and took off at 8.00A for some practice flying with veteran flyer Charlie Decker. A gorgeous morning! "All those people down there," I said, looking down at the cars on U.S. 29, "are missing out big time." "You have to realize," he replied, "that you and I grew up when airplanes were wonderful things. Now, they take second place to smartphones." (Charlie, say it isn't so!)

In 2008 we moved to coastal Georgia (halfway to Miami from Charlottesville), to a place overlooking the tidal inlet of the Herb River, a place like, but not like, Onancock. There are almost daily sightings of the osprey, or fish hawk, a bird that is substantially unchanged after ten million years and presumably at the "peak of perfection." Watching the osprey curving through the air, diving for fish, excites my envy. I read that their daily "time budget" is one or two hours hunting for food, and the rest of the day loafing, preening, perching, resting, sleeping, etc. And, of course flying, for the pure pleasure of it; effortless, it seems. The ideal program!

End

Ch. 20. (C-140). A floatplane allows access to a hundred out-of-the-way places.

APPENDIX

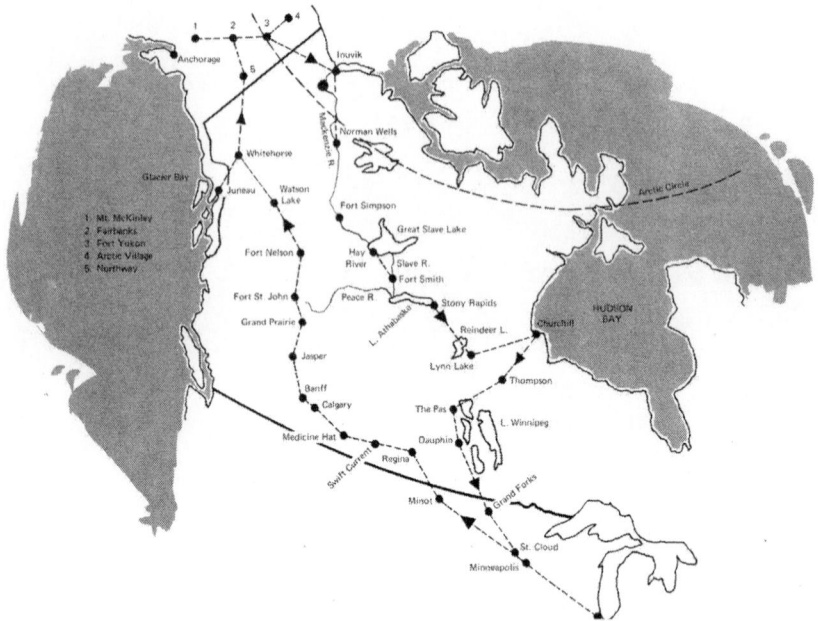

ALASKA/CANADA TRIP 1968

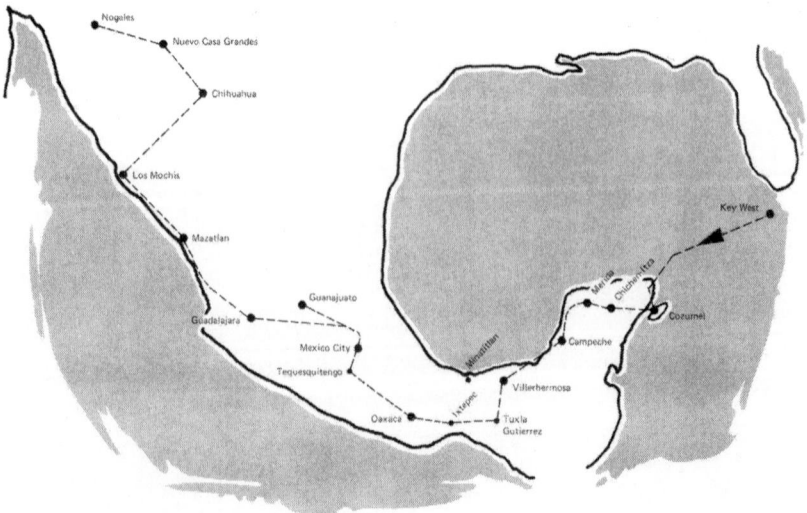

MEXICO TRIP 1969

Anchorage
Inuvik
Norman Wells
Whitehorse
Glacier Bay
Juneau
Watson Lake
Fort Simpson
Mackenzie R.
Arctic Circle
1. Mt. McKinley
2. Fairbanks
3. Fort Yukon
4. Arctic Village
5. Northway
Fort Nelson
Hay River
Great Slave Lake
Slave R.
Fort Smith
Fort St. John
Peace R.
Stony Rapids
Grand Prairie
L. Athabaska
Reindeer L.
Churchill
HUDSON BAY
Jasper
Lynn Lake
Banff
Thompson
Calgary
The Pas
L. Winnipeg
Medicine Hat
Dauphin
Regina
Swift Current
Minot
Grand Forks
St. Cloud
Minneapolis

Nogales
Nuevo Casa Grandes
Chihuahua
Los Mochis
Mazatlan
Guanajuato
Key West
Guadalajara
Mexico City
Merida
Chichen Itza
Cozumel
Tequesquitengo
Minatitlan
Campeche
Oaxaca
Isthmus
Villahermosa
Tuxla Gutierrez

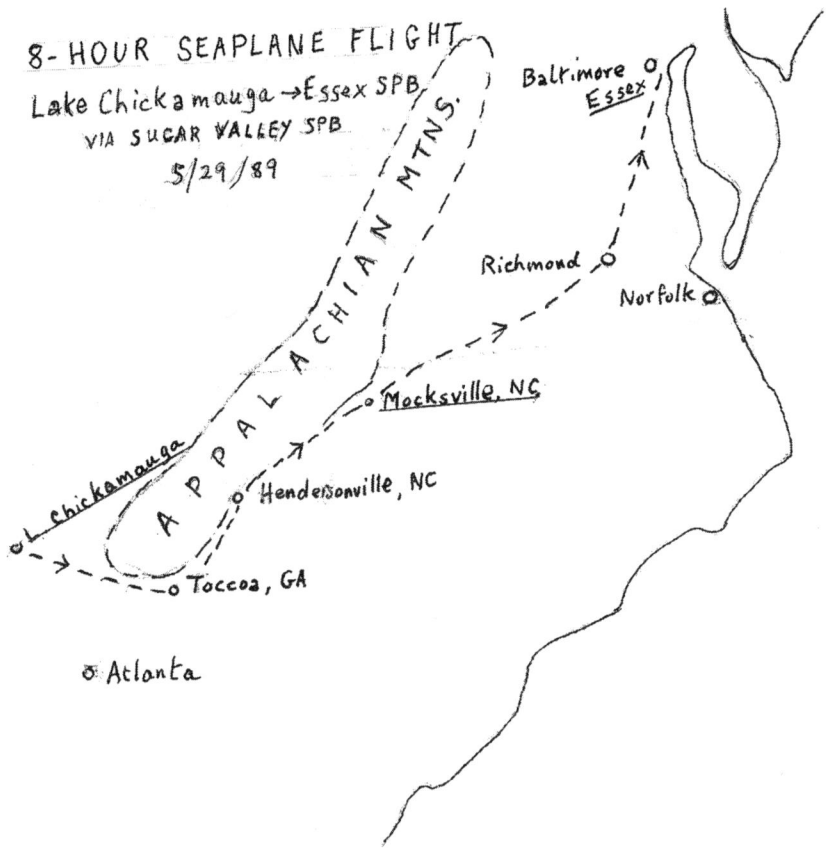

8-HOUR SEAPLANE FLIGHT 1989

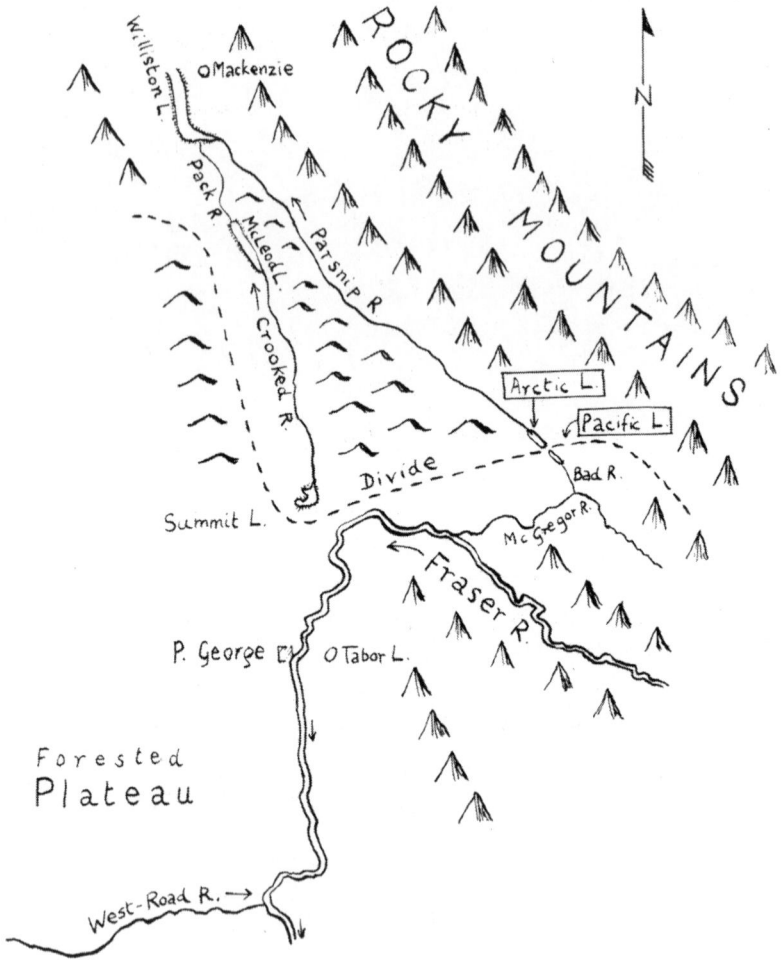

Arctic-Pacific Lakes

Flight of Seaplane N72475 Distances & Times* To:

		St. Mls.	Hrs
0	Back River (Baltimore): Starting Point	—	—
1	Connecticut River (East Haddam)	365	3.5
2	St. Francis River (Drummondville, Que.)	385	3.7
3	Trout Lake (North Bay, Ontario)	395	4.5
4	Wa Wa Lake (Ontario)	370	4.0
5	Lake Superior (Thunder Bay, Ont.)	240	3.0
6	Lake of the Woods (Kenora, Ont.)	340	3.8
7	Icelandic River (Riverton, Manitoba)	170	2.0
8	Grace Lake (The Pas, Man.)	330	4.0
9	Lac La Ronge (Saskatchewan)	260	3.0
10	Churchill Lake (Buffalo Narrows, Sask.)	150	2.0
11	Small Lake (Fort Chipewyan, Sask.)	300	3.7
12	Footner Lake (High Level, Alberta)	250	3.0
13	Charlie Lake (Fort St John, B.C.)	385	3.7
14	Tabor Lake (Prince George, B.C.)	325	3.4
15	Pacific Ocean (Bella Bella, B.C.)	350	3.7
—	Bella Bella & return	—	2.1
16	Campbell River (B.C.)	235	2.5
17	Friday Harbor (San Juan Is., USA)	150	1.6
18	Lake Whatcom (Bellingham, Washington)	35	0.6
	Totals	*5,035*	*57.8*

* includes time on water

185

Coast to Coast Flight Distances

Printed in Great Britain
by Amazon.co.uk, Ltd.,
Marston Gate.